ROUTLEDGE LIBRARY EDITIONS: EDUCATION

SCHOOLS FOR THE BOYS?

SCHOOLS FOR THE BOYS?

Co-education reassessed

PAT MAHONY

Volume 72

Routledge
Taylor & Francis Group

LONDON AND NEW YORK

First published in 1985
Reprinted in 1987

This edition first published in 2012
by Routledge
2 Park Square, Milton Park, Abingdon, Oxfordshire OX14 4RN

Simultaneously published in the USA and Canada
by Routledge
711 Third Avenue, New York, NY 10017

First issued in paperback 2014

Routledge is an imprint of the Taylor and Francis Group, an informa company

British Library Cataloguing in Publication Data
A catalogue record for this book is available from the British Library

ISBN 13: 978-0-415-68359-3 (Volume 72)
ISBN 13: 978-0-415-75066-0 (pbk)

Publisher's Note
The publisher has gone to great lengths to ensure the quality of this reprint but
points out that some imperfections in the original copies may be apparent.

Disclaimer
The publisher has made every effort to trace copyright holders and would
welcome correspondence from those they have been unable to trace.

Schools for the Boys?

Co-education reassessed

Pat Mahony

Hutchinson
in association with
The Explorations in Feminism Collective

London   Melbourne   Sydney   Auckland   Johannesburg

Hutchinson Education

An imprint of Century Hutchinson Ltd

62–65 Chandos Place, London WC2N 4NW
and 51 Washington Street, Dover, New Hampshire 03820, USA

Century Hutchinson Australia Pty Ltd
PO Box 496, 16–22 Church Street, Hawthorn, Victoria 3122, Australia

Century Hutchinson New Zealand Ltd
PO Box 40-086, Glenfield, Auckland 10, New Zealand

Century Hutchinson South Africa (Pty) Ltd
PO Box 337, Bergvlei 2012, South Africa

First published 1985
Reprinted 1987

Set in VIP Plantin by
D. P. Media Limited, Hitchin, Hertfordshire

Printed and bound in Great Britain by
Anchor Brendon Ltd,
Tiptree, Essex

British Library Cataloguing in Publication Data

Mahoney, Pat
  Schools for the boys? : co-education reassessed.
  —(Explorations in feminism)
  1. Women—Education—Great Britain
  I. Title   II. Series
  376'.941   LC2042

Library of Congress Cataloging in Publication Data

Mahony, Pat.
  Schools for the boys.

  (Explorations in feminism;)Bibliography: p.
  1. Coeducation—Great Britain—History.   2. Women—Education
(Secondary)—Great Britain—History.   3. Sex discrimination in education—
Great Britain—Philosophy—History.   4. Sex role—Great Britain—History.
I. Title.   II. Series.
LC1601.M32   1985   367   84–28949

ISBN 0 09 160841 4

Contents

1 Preparing the ground: some general observations on sexism and education

For co-education at secondary school level to be realistically assessed, it has to be put in the context of the historical debates, philosophies and practices about education. To ignore this background is to obliterate the efforts of many people, including women, who genuinely believed that co-education would provide girls with access to some of the educational privileges dispensed to boys. To enable girls to be educated with boys was and still is seen by many as a progressive if not radical move: one which lifted girls' education out of the kitchen and into the modern unisex world. But to be critical of a domestic curriculum for girls and to support co-education are two entirely different things. My research, the techniques and findings of which are discussed in this book, led me to conclude that mixed-sex groupings constitute a disaster area for girls: in what follows I shall try to explain why.

It is not difficult to demonstrate that what survives as 'the history of western political thought' or 'the history of education' contains three rather astonishing features. First, it is the history of men's views: we learn a great deal about John Stuart Mill's general political views, but little if anything about Harriet Taylor Mill's, and this is despite the fact that, on his own admission, much of 'his' work was written together with her (Rossi 1970).* It becomes evident that there is nothing very unusual about this example; women have consistently been 'written off the record' because what they have had to say has often posed a serious challenge to male dominance (Spender 1982), and it is men who control what survives as mainstream knowledge. The problem is not that women have had nothing to say, but rather that what they have said has either been ignored or actively suppressed (Spender 1982).

---

* Full references quoted in the text are contained in the Bibliography beginning on p. 113.

Second, the content of that male history of ideas on education has for the most part been concentrated on boys; where girls have been addressed the commentaries tend to ignore it. Rousseau's reputation as a champion of liberty, for example, rests on his ideas about boys' education – his views on what is right and proper for girls being seldom reported. By the added devices afforded by he/man language (that he means she) the myths are perpetuated that Rousseau was committed to a progressive ideal of education for *children*. But as we can see from the passage quoted below this is not so.

The whole education of women ought to be relative to men. To please them, to be useful to them, to make themselves loved and honoured by them, to educate them when young, to care for them when grown, to counsel them, to console them and to make life sweet and agreeable to them – these are the duties of women at all times and what should be taught them from their infancy.

In my own teacher training I feel that had it been clear that 'man' meant male in the recommended reading on Aristotle on education, or Plato on education, or Herbert Spencer on education, I would have at least been in a position to inquire after females. What I would have discovered might have dramatically altered my attitudes (Okin 1980). This is because what is written about girls' education by these 'great men of ideas' is mostly downright offensive (Mahony 1982).

This brings us to the third feature: that of the specific proposals and general ideology of girls' education. Much excellent research has revealed that a central part of girls' education has always been reserved for their training as wives and mothers within a changing conception of femininity (Dyhouse 1978). The proposals for this training have differed according to the social class of the girls being considered. In the middle to late nineteenth century, middle-class girls were clearly being brought up to perform the managerial task of administering a household.

As with the commander of an army, or the leader of any enterprise, so it is with the mistress of a house. Her spirit will be seen through the whole establishment; and just in proportion as she performs her duties intelligently and thoroughly, so will her domestics follow in her path. (Beaton 1860.)

Working-class girls, on the other hand, received training that prepared them for their future roles as domestic servants. Both groups were being trained for wife and motherhood, although the predicted social class of their future husbands not only made a difference to the nature of that training but also froze a possible social mobility through marriage for working-class girls. Although the norm, this conception of girls' education was resisted by some women:

. . . a girl's education needed to do more than train her for what Maria Grey . . . acidly referred to as the 'button-sewing, soup making, man-pleasing mission of woman'. As early as 1871, Mrs. Grey had argued that girls needed to envisage goals other than marriage in life if they were to take their schooling seriously. (Dyhouse 1978.)

Despite this opposition, the fact remains that although girls' education has not been homogeneous and although there has been active resistance to the whole model from some (mainly women), nevertheless, within state education since 1944, girls' education has been seen largely in terms of their alleged social function. Some government reports have been more explicit than others.

We try to educate girls into becoming imitation men and as a result we are wasting and frustrating their qualities of womanhood at great expense to the community. . . . In addition to their needs as individuals, our girls should be educated in terms of their main social function – which is to make for themselves, their children and their husbands a secure and suitable home and to be mothers. (Newsom 1963.)

It would be simplistic to see Newsom's ideas as having been worked out in any homogeneous way across social class. The 1960s' grammar school girl did far less home economics than her 'less able' peer, though more than her male counterpart who probably did metalwork and woodwork instead.

It is against this historical background that the 'progressive' arguments in favour of co-education have to be understood.[1]* If girls were educated with boys, it was argued, there would be a greater chance that more of them would have access to a decent education which could provide them with more chances to become independent autonomous individuals (Lavigueur 1980).[2] In view of the lamentable lack of facilities in many girls' schools even today (which often only comes to light in the process of amalgamation – schools suddenly find there are

---

* Superior figures refer to the Notes beginning on p. 111.

no CDT workshops for example), it is not difficult to appreciate the progressive intent of the argument.

Achievement or normality

Where there has been any discussion about the educational environment that best suits girls the debate has tended to be set within the parameters of a dilemma. On the one hand, it is often claimed, girls perform better academically in single-sex schools, on the other the world of the co-educational school benefits them socially because it is more 'normal' (Dale 1975).

More recently, doubts have been raised as to whether girls' academic achievement is determined by the presence or absence of boys. It has been suggested, for example, that the social class composition of many girls' schools is more relevant in explaining good results. The research carried out at Banbury School (Postlethwaite and Denton 1980) between streamed and mixed ability co-educational groups adds another dimension. It was reported that there was a marked swing to sciences by the middle ability girls in the unstreamed groups. From this it would appear that ways of grouping girls for learning (independent of any obvious factors relating to social class or single-sex schools) can affect them.

An experiment carried out at Stamford School produced results which suggest that single-sex grouping has an important effect on girls' achievements ('A Question of Equality', BBC2 1981). Girls who were taught on their own in maths for the first two years of secondary schooling performed significantly better than girls of the same ability taught with boys.

But whatever the truth is about the factors contributing to girls' achievement, the preoccupation with the provision of a 'normal' educational environment (for 'normal' read mixed-sex) has figured large even for those convinced of the academic argument. This kind of reasoning sets up a model of the co-educational school as an institution in which girls underachieve academically, but which benefits them socially. In my view, neither of these are true though I shall leave the social arguments until later (see Chapter 2).

The current preoccupation with the underachievement of girls can be questioned on two counts. It is now fashionable to talk of the under-achievement of girls, black pupils and working-class pupils as though these were discrete categories. However, this way of conceptualizing the issue is both racist and sexist for it assumes that girls are white and that black and working-class pupils are boys. Furthermore, this global notion of girls as underachievers is far too simplistic to account for the facts and certainly does not match teachers' experiences. Rather than asking why girls underachieve, which presupposes that they do, whatever the subject and whatever their context for learning, a more sensible line of approach would be to ask: in relation to whom do which girls achieve, in what areas and why? If the question was phrased in this way then perhaps anxiety would begin to be expressed about boys' underachievement in home economics!

Achievement, though of crucial concern, is not the only index by which we ought to be measuring the quality of educational life for girls. The messages girls receive about themselves, and the role school plays in their growth into women are also of vital importance in determining how far girls utilize their abilities both in school and afterwards. It is with these issues in mind that I turn now to review the existing research on girls' schooling which is depressing because it amounts to nothing short of a catalogue of the pressures on girls to become marginal to the educational process.

The content of education

It is not difficult to show that across the whole range of schooling, the content of education as measured by textbooks and other commercially produced material is male, white dominated. If one reviews the many studies that have now been carried out on a range of children's literature, the following picture emerges: in the text and pictures three-quarters of the characters and images are boys and men and one-quarter are girls and women. Lamentably, little of the research reveals that racism is also operative in that of the proportion of females represented, the vast majority are white, living stereotypically white, middle-class lives. Men are depicted in four times as many occupations as women and express themes of achievement and ingenuity; women and girls express dependence and nurturance (Butler and Paisley 1979). This general claim can be confirmed by looking at any specific subject area of the secondary curriculum (apart from home economics). In modern languages, for example, a recent study of examination papers revealed the following:

In the course of various papers from all boards, men and boys appear as doctor, teacher, headteacher, policeman, postman, soldier, concierge, airline pilot, jeweller, thief, traindriver, explorer. They climb mountains, attempt to break records, catch thieves, fish, row boats, almost get drowned or save others from drowning, visit Paris with father, run away from home or get kidnapped. Women and girls ask their husbands for money, make sure the man has a good job before marrying him, prepare food, lay tables, walk quietly because father is working, play the piano and receive orders from men for food and services. (Moys 1980.)

In science, the example quoted below exemplifies a general pattern:

. . . sexist ideology plays its part in terms of illustrations as well as instructions to the students. . . . A picture of Madame Curie with her hand on her husband's shoulder, while he looks down the microscope and she looks at the photographer, allows her contribution to science to be trivialised. (Spender and Sarah 1980.)

In a widely used maths textbook this example was found:

Are you a boy? ——➤ Yes?   Turn to the opposite page.

Here is a flow diagram showing you how
to mix concrete.

No?

Read on

Here is a knitting pattern
for a pullover (Smith 1974).

What is at issue here is not just the assumption that boys are interested in mixing concrete and girls in knitting pullovers, but that for girls their identity is negatively defined in terms of being not boys. One almost expects the text to read: Are you a boy? No? Never mind, we can find something for you to do too.

In poetry, conventionally understood as being of greater interest to females, Margaret Sandra (1982) documents the number of female poets in the anthologies used in her school: twenty-four out of a total of 128.

To cut a very long and tedious story short, the same point can be made whichever subject we choose to analyse (Whyld 1983). That point is that girls are trivialized by and marginalized from the official curriculum to an enormous extent. Moreover, many teachers have found that it is very difficult to challenge this state of affairs in mixed-sex schools (Griffiths 1977; Spender and Sarah 1980). Teachers who try face the prospect of boys' misbehaviour and girls' reluctance to put themselves in the way of humiliating ridicule from boys. A drama teacher writes:

The problem of finding roles which girls can identify with became an acute one for me on Teacher Practice and when I did manage to do so and cast a girl in an important part which might normally have been given to a boy, I found myself feeling *guilty* because I had denied a boy a plum role. Possibly I was also afraid that my choice might cause disruptive behaviour from the boys. Sometimes the boys challenged me, 'Airline pilot? A girl can't be an airline pilot Miss!' Each time this happened I saw the girl hesitate, waiting for my judgement, waiting to be sent back to her seat. 'Of course she can' I would retort, thinking at the same time, 'Can she?' Each time I did this particular lesson, three in all, I cast girls as the pilot and navigator and the boys as the co-pilot. Each time the girl playing the pilot approached me privately, when the others were busy and whispered was I serious? Could women be pilots? Everytime I reassured the girl that it was perfectly alright and would she please go back to her controls before the plane crashed. (Brina 1981.)

But the content of the textbooks to be studied is not the only means by which girls are marginalized. The language used to express that knowledge also tells us that the world is male unless proved otherwise: I am referring of course to the use of 'he' and 'man' to mean 'she' and 'woman'. Dale Spender (1980) has already documented the history of this piece of linguistic skulduggery. She explains that the rationalization that man includes woman is a relatively recent one in the history of the English language. In 1553 a Mr Wilson argued that it was more *natural* to place the man before the woman, and in 1646 a Mr Poole went further by claiming that the male gender was *worthier* and therefore deserved priority. In 1746 a Mr Kirkby invented his 'Eighty Eight Grammatical Rules' with rule twenty-one stating that the male gender was more *comprehensive* than the female. Finally in 1889 an Act of Parliament was passed and 'man' was legally proclaimed to *stand for* 'woman'. If the argument supporting this act were so self-evident why was an Act of Parliament necessary at all?

In June 1981 a notice appeared in the staff bulletin of a London college entitled 'Rules as to Gender'. It read thus:

Members of Academic Board and others who have raised the question of the use of 'he' in College regulations and publications will know that the Dean of Admissions relies for guidance on the Interpretation Act 1889. For those who are unfamiliar with this piece of legislation the relevant section is given below:

In this Act . . words imparting the masculine gender shall include females. (Teacher's Testimony 1981.)

It would be difficult not to see this as a deliberate attempt to write females out of existence, and in spite of the fact that they are apparently in the majority in the college it is unlikely that this situation would be represented on the body to which the Dean is answerable (just as there were no women MPs in 1889). We may be told by men for the next 2000 years that 'man' means 'woman', but nothing will convince me that sentences like 'man is an animal who suckles his young' are sensible. For a group so renowned for its logical prowess this is a sad case of it, for if 'man can suckle his young' (because man includes woman) then man can give birth, become Pope or impregnate man. But this is nonsense, only women can do some of these things and only men others. It is no accident that 'man' does *not* include 'woman' when men's interests are at stake, i.e. a woman cannot become Pope. As the 9-year-old daughter of a friend said, 'It's a trick to pretend they're not leaving us out.'

What this amounts to from the point of view of girls in school is that whatever subject they pursue, the language in which that subject is taught actively excludes them. In view of the sensitivity on the part of most teachers to the issues of language as a potential barrier to the education of working-class children it is deplorable that when asked to consider the same issue from the point of view of girls the most common reaction (in my experience) is to nod and then ignore it or to accuse us of triviality. But of course it is not trivial: for women there is always a decoding exercise to be done to find out whether or not we are included. The he/man language always includes men; women are only included some of the time.

Furthermore, it would seem that young children are unaware that 'man means woman', so for them the world is being represented as more male than it actually is. Studies involving older students have shown time and again that when asked to design a book cover for 'Man and His World' they drew men, whereas when asked to do the same task for a text entitled 'People and their World' both sexes are represented (Nilsen 1972; Hacker and Schneider 1972).

The fact that there is space available in girls' schools to at least partially rectify what amounts to a gross distortion of reality does not mean that nothing can be done in mixed schools. The DASI Project co-ordinated by Annie Cornbleet and Sue Sanders (see p. 77), funded by ILEA and the EOC, gives clear guidelines as to the kind of things that might be done in co-educational institutions (I shall discuss this later when I consider 'strategies').

One further point must be made about content before moving on to other aspects of the curriculum. Distorted and offensive though it may be, riddled with he/man language though it still is, despite the information on the subject (Spender 1980), no straightforward links can be made between biased, sexist material and girls' alleged underachievement. First, the same textbooks are used in single-sex schools and the contents are not always challenged by teachers. Second, it is not true that girls underachieve across the board in education. Relative to boys they achieve highly in English and modern languages, yet as we have seen the curriculum in these areas is no less biased in favour of males. As I have suggested, girls' underachievement in schools is neither a useful nor accurate way of theorizing the problem, as we shall see in the next section.

Who does what in schools? – pupils

Figures 1–3 show that the problem does not begin with who achieves in what, but rather with the subjects that the pupils either choose or are entered for. These figures reflect the national picture and speak for themselves. Figure 4 shows that at all levels in London a greater proportion of boys take physics and chemistry and a greater proportion of girls take French and biology. At A-level, more boys take maths and more girls take English. The division is even sharper in technical subjects (see Figure 5).

In achievement, however, the situation is rather different. As far as we can tell from limited data, girls achieve better grades than boys at all examination levels (ILEA 1981, see Figure 6). In English, the situation regarding girls' achievement is even more startling:

Whilst girls, on the basis of examination results, are judged to do badly in the maths, science area, little attention has been paid to the excellent results achieved by girls in English. Over 45,000 more girls than boys passed O. Level in 1979 and they repeated this success in Literature O. Level by just under 40% extra passes. This was on an entry percentage difference of approximately 9% in both examinations. (Sandra 1982.)

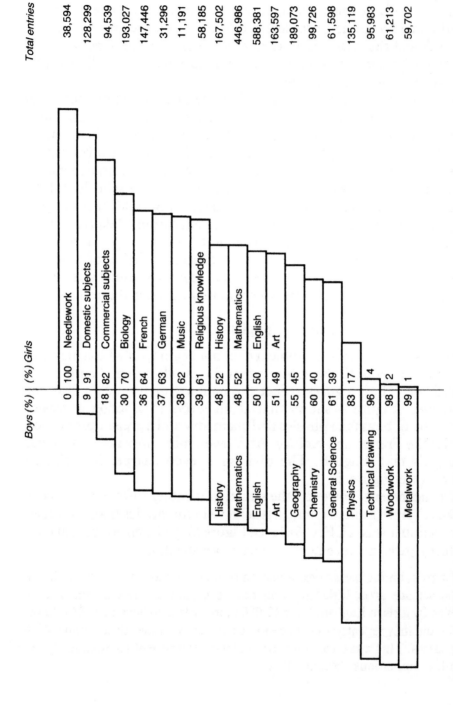

Figure 1 The percentage distribution of boys and girls in CSE (all modes) entries (1980)
Source: The GATE Project, Chelsea College.

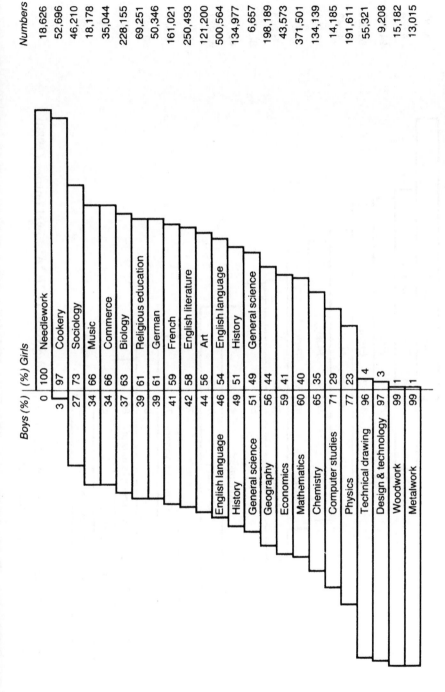

	Boys (%)	(%) Girls		Numbers
	0	100	Needlework	18,626
	3	97	Cookery	52,696
	27	73	Sociology	46,210
	34	66	Music	18,178
	34	66	Commerce	35,044
	37	63	Biology	228,155
	39	61	Religious education	69,251
	39	61	German	50,346
	41	59	French	161,021
	42	58	English literature	250,493
	44	56	Art	121,200
English language	46	54	English language	500,564
History	49	51	History	134,977
General science	51	49	General science	6,657
Geography	56	44		198,189
Economics	59	41		43,573
Mathematics	60	40		371,501
Chemistry	65	35		134,139
Computer studies	71	29		14,185
Physics	77	23		191,611
Technical drawing	96	4		55,321
Design & technology	97	3		9,208
Woodwork	99	1		15,182
Metalwork	99	1		13,015

Figure 2 The percentage distribution of boys and girls in GCE 'O' Level entries (summer 1980)
Source: The GATE Project, Chelsea College.

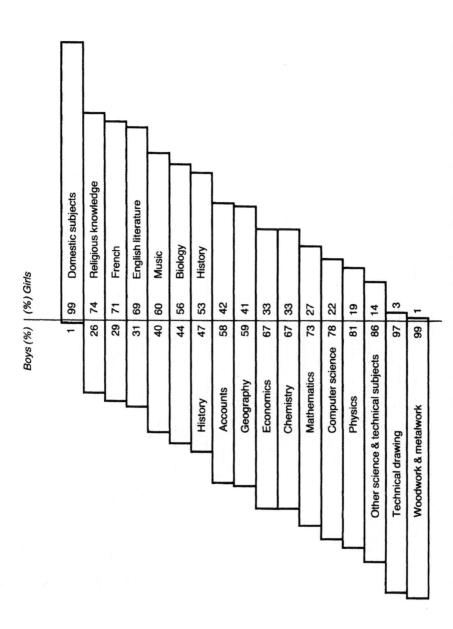

Figure 3 The percentage distribution of boys and girls in GCE 'A' Level entries (1980)
Source: The GATE Project, Chelsea College.

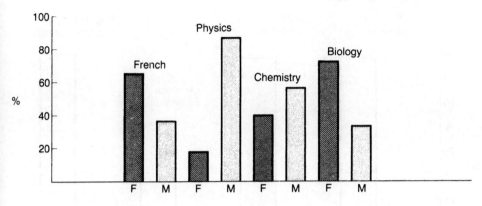

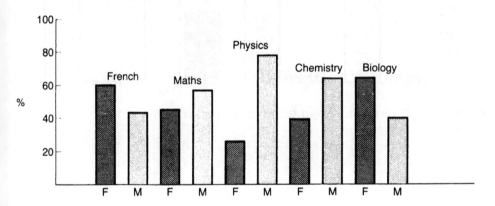

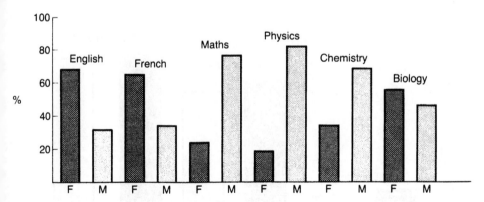

Figure 4　CSE entries in England (1979)
　'O' Level entries in England (1979)
　'A' Level entries in England (1979)

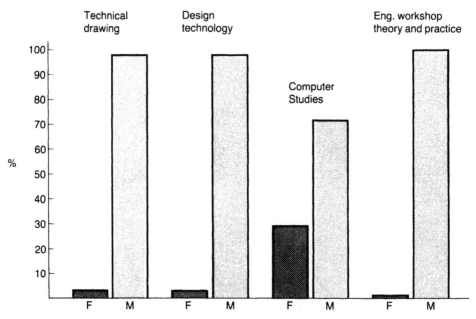

Figure 5   'O' Level entries in technical subjects (1979)
Source: ILEA 1981.

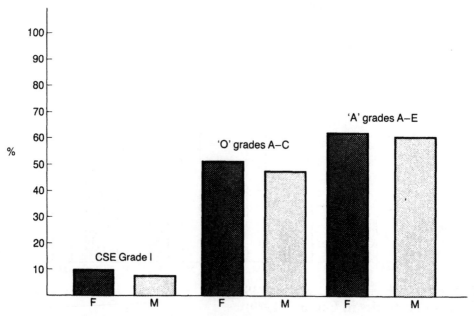

Figure 6   ILEA examination results (1980)

Three main issues arise from these facts. First, girls' ability is clearly not at issue. The Inner London Education Authority reports that:

Female candidates did well in those subjects where the proportion entering was small. In Physics for example, although girls accounted for only 15% of C.S.E. entries a slightly greater proportion than boys achieved grade 1; at 'O' level where only 29% of entries were female, almost identical proportions of boys and girls gained grades A to C. (ILEA 1981.)

Second, the patterning of girls' subject 'choices' and the extent to which, in relation to boys, they are *not entered* for public examinations in certain subjects *is* the issue. Third, whatever accounts for these patterns, the Stamford school experiment suggests that the presence of boys is a relevant factor in girls' performance in maths (Figure 7). One of the factors at work in this division of the curriculum is the obvious contradiction for girls between femininity and academic success: '. . . femininity and individual achievements which reflect intellectual competence or leadership potential are desirable but mutually exclusive goals' (Horner 1972). This contradiction is sharpened by the labelling of some subjects such as maths and science as 'masculine' or 'hard' subjects in comparison with others such as English and modern languages which are defined as 'feminine' or 'soft' subjects (Deem 1978; MacDonald 1980). But again these general factors are not sufficient to explain why there is greater rigidity of subject choice in a mixed-sex school: why 'Girls are more likely to choose a science and boys a

| | Test marks (per cent) | | |
	Oct 1978	Nov 1979	Feb 1980
All girls set	59	55	55
Girls in equivalent mixed set	58	50	44
Boys in equivalent mixed set	59	59	56

Figure 7   Stamford School Experiment

language in a single sex school than they are in a mixed school.' (DES 1975.)

Anne-Marie Wolpe's research (1977) suggests that one factor in this is the ridicule which pupils fear from each other if they make unconventional choices. Left to 'choose' they will play safe in line with traditional sex-role expectations. This may suggest that the pressures on girls and boys are equal and similar (a highly questionable assumption!). In terms of my own experience in classrooms I would expect the majority of the pressure on boys and girls to come from boys. Furthermore, a girl wanting to do carpentry rather than cookery is operating out of gender role whereas a boy choosing cookery may do so in terms of realistic career ambitions – he may want to become a chef.

What is at issue on this point is not that we are obsessed with trying to make boys and girls the same (an accusation which is often made) but rather that what is 'chosen' by boys gives them access to a wider range of more highly paid jobs. For example, girls tend to cluster in biology, boys in physical sciences, but as Diana Leonard (1977) points out:

Unfortunately biology as a single science at Ordinary level is not very useful, either as a qualification for further education or for general use outside school. And you certainly can't go on to higher level science or medicine or whatever without physical sciences.

At this point in the discussion it is necessary to assess the relevance of the debate concerning girls' achievements. The matter is not straightforward.

First, it is relevant in the face of any argument which supposes that girls as a group underachieve (especially if this assumption leads to questions concerning the size of the female brain). Second, it is relevant to show that girls' achievement in mixed-sex schools varies with the subject they do and is not entirely dependent on the presence of boys. It is important to do this because it is not good enough for science and maths staff to attribute the problem to the unchangeable nature of girls' lowered expectations in mixed-sex contexts. Third, it must be acknowledged that over and above the mixed-sex/single-sex issue a very complicated network of factors operate when we try to analyse girls' achievement; specific conceptions of femininity which may vary with race, social class and culture and definitions of subjects as 'masculine' or 'feminine'.

However, there is a danger in girls' achievement becoming the issue with which we become preoccupied. This would be a mistake because the social issue also needs to be assessed. Here we need to ask not only, 'why is co-education socially desirable, what do girls learn from it?', but also 'what do they do with their qualifications once having left school?' For example, are the expectations of girls educated in mixed-sex schools different from those of girls educated in single-sex schools?

Who does what in school? – teachers

The position of women teachers in schools is not exactly conducive to girls being given role models which might challenge their lowered expectations; and as more schools become co-educational the position worsens. Women represent a high proportion of teachers compared with other professions: 59 per cent in 1978, but are grossly under-represented at the top of the profession. In 1981 4.4 per cent of women were head teachers as against 10 per cent of men. On the lowest scale, however, the situation was dramatically reversed: 39.2 per cent of women as compared with 19.2 per cent of men (EOC 1981). Although it was not revealed by the research, it is undoubtedly the case that the majority of women who do gain promotion are white: thus for black women and women of colour there are two discriminations at work – sex and race.

According to conventional wisdom, the explanation of the domination by men of the top of the profession is that promotion is available but women are not interested in it. However, a recent report suggests that:

There is absolutely no evidence for the myth of the 'strikingly low promotion orientation' of women teachers. The majority of our respondents considered themselves to be career oriented and would welcome the challenge and wider responsibilities that promotion would bring. There was no evidence whatsoever that marriage and/or the acquisition of a family alter this attitude. Those supporting a family single handed were, naturally, particularly concerned about the financial rewards of promotion. Nonetheless, despite their overall career orientation, women teachers do have difficulties in gaining promotion. Our analysis of the experiences of our respondents in applying for promotion led us to the inescapable conclusion that a fair measure of discrimination does indeed exist. (EOC/NUT 1980.)

There is evidence to show that the situation is becoming worse. The

Women's National Commission recently produced a report which demonstrated that the proportion of headships filled by women has dropped from 25 per cent to 16 per cent over the last twenty years. Among the eighty-six local education authorities who responded, eight had no women heads at all and in another twenty-nine less than 10 per cent of heads were women. The decline is mainly ascribed to the diminishing number of single-sex schools. A woman is much less likely to be appointed to head a mixed school than a man, the report says, although men are quite frequently appointed as heads of girls' schools (*TES* 1983a).

A survey by Inner London Education Authority (*TES* 1984a) found that another factor contributing to the lack of promotion for women teachers was that 'women were more likely to have been refused permission to attend courses'. As an Education Authority with a current record far better than most, ILEA is not without its critics. A male head said: 'It's a definite advantage to be a woman at the moment. We will be watching the situation closely and obviously we'll be worried if there is an imbalance in any way.' (*TES* 1984b.) It is revealing that this head does not see fit to worry about the imbalance of the last 2000 years or even of the current overall situation in which women do not enjoy equal promotion with men. It seems that if attempts are made to make opportunities more equal, men perceive them as discriminatory.

It becomes evident that although girls in single-sex schools are not free from the constraints imposed by the biased content of education, from the he/man language in which it is framed, from the contradictions between femininity and academic success, or from the models of status, power and authority generated by the structuring of female and male career patterns, their situation is consistently better than that of their counterparts in mixed-sex schools. With this in mind I turned my attention to the research which has been done on mixed-sex groupings. If the situation seems worse I asked, what is it about co-education that makes it allegedly more desirable? Unfortunately, in my subsequent search for an answer to this question, I was unable to discover anything advantageous for girls, although I found a great deal that was beneficial to boys.

Boys' monopoly of physical space

An obvious place to begin a review of the research on mixed-sex situations is with an analysis of the amount of physical space occupied by boys, in relation to girls. In a study in 1977, Anne-Marie Wolpe found that the playground was monopolized by boys.

What happens in the mixed playground is that boys monopolise almost the total area by playing football, while the girls sit around on benches or wander round the periphery. Some, at great risk, pick their way across the football pitch, but few would dare to do so. There are in fact no chances for girls to participate or to be physically active during the school breaks. Their own quiet playground precludes this as all balls are banished from it. . . .

Even though a number of girls during the course of their interviews expressed a desire to join in, when asked why they did not do so they laughed at the stupidity of the question. It simply was not feasible – they would be howled down by the boys.

Seven years later, a group of student teachers investigating the use of physical space in one mixed school arrived at similar conclusions:

We decided to take these photographs after being somewhat shocked through our own research at the stark truth of Anne-Marie Wolpe's research. We think they represent the appropriation of space by boys. Not only are the original observations confirmed, but also the situation has not changed despite awareness amongst staff. In fact, we were able to find no counter instances.

From our observations we offer the following conclusions:

Girls tend to spend their lunch hour in small groups of two to four tucked away where they are inconspicuous

Boys can be seen to walk directly into or across large open areas, while girls walk around the footpaths which hug the buildings

Boys occupy large areas of physical space in the playground while the girls sit around the edges

Girls are often found in the role of spectator; they sit and watch the boys' activities

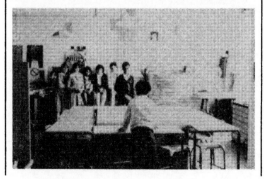

Boys' activities commonly involve large groups and are of a faster and more violent nature

When girls play 'active' games they use less of the available space than boys

When girls are in a group, they still take up less space than boys

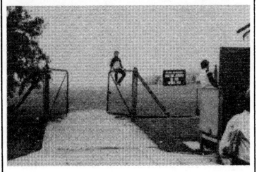

Boys regularly appropriate space by climbing on each other and structures other than seats

We are not saying that these roles are natural, because before the boys arrived at the site of this school, the large open spaces were used by the girls. Boys have monopolised and taken spaces which they feel to be theirs. Girls have not resisted in this instance other than by forming small groups and moving away. (Wildy, Howe, Crosbie, Collins and Berman 1984.)

My own impressions of the situation inside the classroom correspond with these observations. Although I have not checked with a tape measure, it does seem that the space assumed by boys to be theirs is far greater than that occupied by girls. Boys not only 'spread' into gangways and spaces around their own desks (which are often the ones most central to the teacher), but they also appear not to notice that space is already occupied by girls. It is not uncommon to find a boy leaning across a girl's desk in order to 'flick' another boy, crumpling her work in the process. Neither is it uncommon, when this behaviour is challenged, to encounter a reaction of amazement and incomprehension from the boys. It is apparently usual for them to not notice the physical presence of girls, nor to consider it important to do so.

Boys' monopoly of linguistic space

A second area of considerable concern, given the importance of pupil talk in the learning process, is the way in which linguistic space is dominated by boys. Research undertaken by Zimmerman and West (1975) showed that in male/female conversations nearly all the interruptions (94 per cent) were by men and that females were more silent than males. Dale Spender (1978) found that girls and boys receive different messages about themselves through the processes of linguistic interaction. These are that it is:

1   normal for the teacher to ignore the girls for long periods of time, but not the boys;
2   normal for boys to call out, move from their seats, push each other;
3   normal for girls to be addressed collectively, boys by their individual names;
4   normal for boys to dominate classroom talk;
5   normal for boys to talk rough and girls to talk soft.

Jenny Gubb (1980) found, in addition, that girls are more likely to offer support in discussion. Four years later little had changed. Luise

Horrocks (1984) found that men dominated mixed-sex talk not by quantity alone. She analysed the discussions of seven student teacher groups engaged in a code cracking exercise. She found not only that men talk more than women but also that women: 'pause more often and do not exclude others by occupying time. If a person wished to contribute, s/he would have more room to do so where there is a greater amount of pause'. And: 'Men seemed to occupy "centre stage" much more readily than women. The longest time of any of the tapes that a woman spoke uninterrupted by a man was 49 seconds. The longest time a man spoke uninterrupted was 2 minutes 28 seconds.' Lengths of between twenty and forty seconds were consistently recorded for male speech whereas female sequences lasted very often for only one or two seconds. She goes on to explain that

It seems to me that men establish their 'right' to talk longer by leading the conversation from the beginning and in the process establishing its framework. . . . This sense of natural and automatic leadership that men have pervades all the tapes. On the solving of the code in one group a male voice is heard to say 'Well done team!' We can only suppose that the man in question consciously or otherwise sees himself as the leader of the group and in a position to praise the others for their efforts. It was in fact a woman who did most of the code cracking.

She continues:

A man says 'That's the system, I'm telling you, that's the system'. Not only do the words themselves subordinate, but the tone in which they are uttered is enough to prevent this particular woman from participating much more – a shame because the system that this man had constructed was totally wrong.

Boys' monopoly of teacher attention

It has been found that the boys in a mixed-sex class get roughly two-thirds of the teacher attention (Spender 1980). This situation does not always follow from a lack of awareness of the problem. Vivienne Griffiths (1977) writes:

I am fully aware that during my own lessons, I frequently treated girls and boys differently: it is remarkably difficult to break through behaviour seen as the norm. For example, when a group of loudly disruptive boys threatened to reduce a whole class to chaos it often seemed simpler and less wearing to focus attention and content on them and try to prevent further disturbance than to stick to principles about 'not paying more attention to the boys'.

This experience is not peculiar to secondary school teachers. In her research on primary schools, Katherine Clarricoates (1976) found a similar situation: 'The boys are more difficult to settle down to their work . . . they don't seem to have the same self-discipline as the girls do, so it's important to direct the subject at them.' And: 'It's important to keep their attention . . . otherwise they play you up something awful.' Since the professional competence of teachers is partly judged in terms of skills in class management and control, the dilemma about whether to opt for equal attention for boys and girls or whether to risk uproar, is a very real one.

Teachers' attitudes to pupils

Michelle Stanworth's research supports the findings outlined in the previous section. She goes on to investigate teachers' attitudes to girls and boys. She presents data which show that for every four boys who participated in classroom discussion, there was one girl. For every two boys who asked questions there was one girl: three boys to one girl received praise and encouragement, and in these classes (A-level English) there were more girls than boys. Both the girls and the boys stated that teachers are more concerned about boys, that they consider the boys more conscientious and capable, that they get on better with the boys and that they are twice as likely to consider boys as the model pupils.

In the light of what educationalists claim about the importance of teacher expectation in the educational process this constitutes a serious situation from the point of view of girls. Of a girl considering a career in law, a teacher said: 'I can imagine her being a very competent secretary. She looks neat and tidy, her work's neat and tidy, she's perfectly prompt at arriving.' (Stanworth 1983.) Of another girl who intended to qualify as a psychologist: 'I can imagine her being a nurse.' And by way of a final straw:

Interviewer: 'What course might suit her then?'
Teacher: 'I can't really say. I don't really know about jobs for girls.'

Michelle Stanworth goes on to show not only how some teachers view pupils but also that girls know what their teachers think of them. More worrying still is the suggestion that the teacher's view is internalized:

Female Pupil: I think he thinks I'm pretty mediocre. I think I'm pretty mediocre. He never points me out of the group, or talks to me, or looks at me in particular when he's talking about things. I'm just a sort of wallpaper person. (Stanworth 1983.)

For anyone not committed to the slow demise of half the population there is nothing which could remotely be described as socially desirable for girls in the findings above. Quite simply they do not get their fair share of teachers' attention or of educational space and they receive messages suggesting they are less valued than boys.

In the light of this evidence, the only remaining way in which co-educational schools could benefit girls is in the interaction of the peer group. Some existing research concentrating on boys' attitudes to girls suggests that it is not a promising line of inquiry. Jenny Shaw (1977) has argued that boys in mixed-sex classrooms seek to emphasize their masculinity by being as unlike the girls as possible: they use the girls as a negative reference group. Michelle Stanworth's documentation of boys' comments about girls confirms this suggestion:

In reply to the question, 'Who would you least wish to be like?', all of the boys named the girls (and only girls). It must be emphasised that the characteristic of female pupils most vehemently rejected by boys is the apparent marginality of girls in classroom encounters. The term 'faceless', used time and time again by boys (but by none of the girls) to describe their female classmates, seems to sum up boys' feeling that silence robs the girls of any claim to individual identity and respect.

Two other pieces of research were available to me prior to my beginning the more detailed inquiry into the interaction between boys and girls in school. Neither disposed me to think that I would find in that interaction those features which allegedly make co-education desirable for girls. One piece of research was conducted by a drama teacher who monitored the content of her lesson:

There is a good deal of abusive language used mainly by boys towards girls in their improvisations. In one day I collected the following insults, used while acting and no doubt considered by the boys who used them as essential to the action. In fact, looking back at the notes which I made at the time, I realise that these insults *were* essential to the action. How else could the boys have conveyed what they felt about women?

'this bird who can't get a boyfriend'
'you dopey cow'
'silly cow' (five times)
'you're a woman aint ya' (to a cowardly boxer)
'you tart' (the boy was acting beating up the girl prior to raping her)
'she's not even pretty' (one girl to another about a third who was supposed to be stupid).

(Brina 1981.)

The teacher subsequently documented the activities chosen during one lesson

. . . in which the brief was to work out a physical trick which depended on careful timing and group work:
1   woman being 'touched up' at the bus stop and subsequently hitting the wrong man;
2   a boxing match, in which there being no role for the girl in the group, she simpered around playing a hostess;
3   *two* women being 'touched up' in the park by the same man;
4   a bank robbery which failed because one of the robbers (a girl) broke her fingernail and delayed everyone;
5   yet another woman being 'touched up', this time on a train.

She comments on this:

I did not hear any of the girls use any corresponding terms of abuse for a boy. But what pejoratives are there which can be used against a male which are equivalent of 'cow', 'bitch', 'tart', 'bird', and 'scrubber', all of which I heard at some time in my lessons. There is one which the boys assured me that girls sometimes used against them and which I knew they used against each other and that is 'poof'. It is apparently the worst insult to compare a boy with someone who is considered feminine.

In the other piece of research, which was conducted by Carabin and Dodd (1982), boys were interviewed about their attitudes to women teachers as part of a wider study on the sexual harassment of female staff. Time and again boys complain that if they were in a mixed school, women teachers 'wouldn't get it'. Whether or not women in mixed schools are subject to less sexual harassment than women in boys' schools is hardly the point. Rather it is that if the boys interviewed assumed that the absence of girls caused women teachers to be harassed then this could only mean that if girls were present they would become the primary targets. The boys saw it as a problem only in as much as they felt teachers to be inappropriate targets and since this was a situation not of their making they resented any criticism.

In case it is assumed that all this operates at the level of boys' fantasy (which would be bad enough) there are a growing number of reports which illustrate the reality of the situation:

Obscene comments varied from a first year boy saying 'Miss is this your last day, can we feel you up' to boys making lewd comments if I was ever seen walking out of a room with a male member of staff. One fourth year boy spent *every* lesson drawing obscene pictures of me – this was laughed at not dealt with. (Student Teacher 1983.)

In the course of my own teaching I asked students how the lecture on 'Sexism' could be improved and I received this reply:

While I was on Teaching Practice a female member of staff was sexually assaulted by six 4th year boys. Three of them were suspended for a few days and now they are back in school. Many times boys warned me not to push things too far – 'you know what happened to Miss T . . .' they would say. I felt last term's course probably did not stress enough how to handle situations of a more serious nature. What do you do if a boy calls you a slag, assaults you, makes obscene suggestions? Why is the higher authority referred to always a man? Why do women teachers feel scared of some of their pupils? Why are they forced to be aware of them as a physical threat? These are some of the questions in my mind now. (Student Teacher 1983.)

So it was, with all this primary research behind me that I began to investigate the interaction between boys and girls in co-educational schools. This was the only feature of the system left that could be beneficial to girls. I did not expect to find a paradise of blossoming egalitarian relationships given the information I already had, but neither was I prepared for what I found.

2 A can of worms: the sexual harassment of girls by boys

It is difficult to define the exact period of time during which the research was conducted. Since one of the most significant features of the whole venture is the process by which the material was gathered it is perhaps worth telling the story in full.

I began observing the interaction between boys and girls while supervising students on teaching practice. Although over two full terms this provided a rich source of information (at one time I had over 300 diagrams of seating arrangements in classrooms) and enabled me to derive some organizing categories for the material, I was uneasy about gathering data in this way. It raised questions about the ethics of using my legitimate access to schools and classrooms for quite another purpose. First, I felt that I was not giving my full attention to the students although, for some, their responses, had I sought them, may not have been wholly negative! More fundamentally, having become interested in the matter I could not help noticing what went on and I felt very uncomfortable about using such information since I had not gained permission to gather it. Schools are quite understandably sensitive about the practices of researchers, having had their fill of distorted and inaccurate representations which make the teaching staff appear as a bunch of incompetent buffoons. Because I felt it very important to obtain permission to undertake my research, I burnt the notes I had made. This left me with a framework for a research project.

Equipped with this framework I approached several schools in different parts of London. Typically as co-educational schools they all had male heads and, in going through the list of schools in London, I was struck by the fact that many had men's names but hardly any were named after women.[1]

I chose three schools that I regarded as being fairly representative of their kind: one on the outskirts of London was a purpose-built co-educational comprehensive school with a high proportion of white middle-class children; another was a small inner-city ex-grammar school with a wide racial and social-class mix; and the third had originally been a girls' school which many of the staff remembered. I spent time in each school (with the Head's permission), observing classes, talking to teachers and to students. I found a marked difference in awareness of and concern for the girls in the school which had previously been all girls. The staff, in general, recognized the changes that had occurred in girls' access to education and many did not like what they saw. The concern, which at times was expressed with considerable emotion, is best communicated by the head of science:

'Before we went mixed the girls used to be really interested in science, they used to love doing the experiments and working out why things happened. Now they don't get a look in, the boys rush in and collar all the equipment. I waste hours hauling them off. Now the girls just hang around. I just don't understand it. I wonder if it's biological or something.'
Int: 'How can it be though? You said it didn't used to be like that.'
Teacher: 'I know, I'm really confused about it, it makes me so angry to see *our* girls going this way.' (My emphasis.)

This teacher, having experienced the girls' behaviour when the school was single sex, perhaps continued to see the school as a girls' school and thus was not typical of male teachers who generally seem to regard the situation described above as normal (though faintly undesirable). For him it was the change which he perceived as having occurred in girls' learning which made the difference.

After having visited the three schools fairly regularly over a number of weeks 'the research' as an activity carried out on a limited sample over a quantifiable time came to an abrupt halt. This was because I began talking about my findings to other people: during workshops at conferences, in seminars at my own and other colleges in different parts of the country, at teachers' centres, and informally with colleagues and friends. Whenever possible I taped these discussions and I always asked to be sent any relevant information. The response over a period of about six months was literally overwhelming: diaries of 'a typical week' (or in some cases a day was enough), tape recordings of discussions between groups of girls and descriptions of isolated incidents were sent, mainly by women teachers and girls. The original framework collapsed under this deluge and with it my neat plan of points to be made and evidence to back them. It was when I began to receive correspondence from

Hungary, Holland and the United States of America that I realized things had got out of hand. Assuming that a lack of information is always a problem in research, the other extreme of being drowned in it is equally difficult.

What follows then is not 'my research' but an attempt to group into themes a great deal of information from a large number of people, some of whom I have never met, some whose full names I do not know. The account is in no way meant to be an exhaustive description of mixed-sex schooling. Rather it is an alarm bell to which teachers may respond by talking to girls, keeping diaries and discussing with each other as a preliminary to developing strategies for change.

The mixed-sex classroom

On the face of it boys and girls seem to pay little sustained attention to each other in the mixed-sex classsroom. Rarely did school students report friendships with members of the opposite sex and where they did express a liking for each other and even a desire to be friends it was often felt that other pupils would interpret this as more than friendship. Sometimes boys expressed their anxiety that their masculinity would be threatened if they showed interest in having a girl as a friend in school, although for older boys masculinity was enhanced by having a girl friend provided she was a girl popular with other boys (here the emphasis was more on competition with other boys than on the relationship with the girl). The younger girls did not express any loss of status by being friends with a boy, although many said they had little interest in developing such relationships and preferred the company of other girls because: 'Most boys act stupid', and 'Girls talk about things better.' Younger girls often resented what they perceived as an accusation that they 'loved' particular boys. Evidence that this is not confined to secondary schools came from this 9-year-old girl. As a budding gymnast she was described by the teacher as being much 'admired' by the boys. Her interpretation was somewhat different:

'The boys keep on about which one I love but I don't love any of them and I tell them but they don't take any notice. It's really embarrassing, I don't like it. Ben bought me a Christmas present but I wouldn't take it because they would have said I love him and I don't. I think Miss P. is cross with me for being rude because I heard her talking about it with Ben's Mum. Now they're saying I look like a boy.'

Int: 'What do you say to that?'
Girl: 'You look like a skunk.'

Older girls were careful to avoid 'going out with' boys who might give them a bad reputation but on the other hand many felt that not dating a boy at all could be equally problematic in raising questions and comments about their sexuality. One girl whose main interest in life was horse riding reported a number of crude comments concerning her preference for the animals' company to that of the boys. There is already much documentation of the complicated manoeuvres which girls have to practice if they are to even begin negotiating the 'slags and drags' dichotomy (McRobbie and McCabe 1981; Hemmings 1982).

Although this material is not the central concern of this study, it forms the background to the situation in which teachers perceive there to be little interaction between girls and boys. This assumption that girls and boys inhabit separate worlds in the mixed classroom is not surprising when one looks at diagrams of seating arrangements. Over and over again, examples can be found of boys dominating the teacher's field of vision and of girls occupying marginal positions. Thus what is at issue is not just the marked physical separation of girls and boys but also the fact of boys' dominance in the class. However, the assumption of separateness, though in this sense supported by the evidence, turned out to be totally false: there is a great deal of interaction in the mixed-sex classroom. Despite the fact that many boys reported that they 'don't bother with the girls' and although boys do not consider girls when ranking themselves academically (Stanworth 1983), there is in fact a great deal of 'bothering'. An enormous amount of time and energy is expended by boys in what amounts in the end to the social control of girls. There are numerous examples which differ slightly in detail, but a number of recurring themes emerge from the material.

Style and gesture in the classroom

Often boys do not have to say anything in order to convey to the girls in class that their participation in the lesson is unwelcome:

Fifth-year girl: 'It's very subtle really – whenever a girl speaks in more than one-word answers the atmosphere gets tense, the boys don't really like it.'
Int: 'How do you know?'
Girl: 'Well they put their pens down – you know – time for a break. If she

carries on they fold their arms, lean back in their chair and – sort of – look deliberately bored. Do you know what I mean?'

Sometimes 'acting bored' is accompanied by sound:

Third-year girl: 'The boys always act bored whenever a girl says anything in class. It doesn't matter what she says. She's soon drowned down with groaning and sighing.'

Many girls were defensive about admitting their difficulties in participating in lessons. Comments like: 'I could talk if I wanted to', or 'I prefer to get on with my work', were common. One problem is to disentangle girls' 'choice' not to participate in discussion from a more general phenomemon in which school students fail to see discussion as work.

The initial interviews which I conducted were very tortured. In order not to ask 'leading questions' I asked more general ones, but in doing so I repeatedly found myself engaged in a fascinating dialogue about the relationship between thought and speech. In the end it was easier to simply ask students what they thought of the claim that 'Boys prevent girls taking part in class discussions' or to show a clip of a video in which girls say that 'Boys put girls down in class.' Avoidance of ridicule was cited over and over again in these sessions as the girls' reason for not participating in lessons. They did not always specifically cite the boys as the source of this ridicule:

Second-year girl: 'I always think twice before I say anything in class because the others laugh at you.'
Int: 'Which others, is it always the same ones?'
Girl: 'Well mostly, it's David and Michael T. who make fun of you but the other boys grin.'

As has already been indicated, many of the younger girls saw the behaviour of the boys as less controlling:

First-year girl: 'I think some of the boys are really stupid. They don't like girls being good at their work and they try to laugh at you but I don't take any notice of them – they're stupid. My Mum says they won't be laughing when they can't get a job.'

Apart from the support which this girl had from her mother who apparently regretted leaving university to get married (the girl told me), her comment seems to confirm what many primary school teachers say about girls having no hesitation in 'giving as good as they get'. It is also interesting to consider whether younger girls experience pressure to express their femaleness through particular versions of femininity, which are at odds with qualities of 'intelligence' or 'cleverness'.

There is little automatic support among the girls for each other, a situation which some female teachers have sought to redress by setting up girls' groups (often with considerable opposition).

Fourth-year girl: 'You must be joking Miss. I never open my mouth. Anyway no-one's interested. The boys start chit-chatting between themselves and the girls start getting edgy that any minute one of the boys is going to start getting faisty.'

Sometimes an even stronger claim is made, that boys' behaviour is provoked by the girls. This next comment is uncomfortably close to the kind of 'blame the victim' model in which women are ultimately held responsible for male violence:

Third-year girl: 'No, I don't think boys and girls are different in class – it's just a certain group who make fun of everyone.'
Int: 'Who are they?'
Girl: 'Mostly it's Gary, Roy and Denis – sometimes Peter T. but he's away a lot.'
Int: 'Who do they make fun of?'
Girl: 'Well not me because I don't say much but Angela's always going on and so is Tracy. They think they're it, they ask for it.'

This comment does, of course, raise other questions. It is not clear whether the boys mentioned make fun of everyone as she suggests at the beginning or only of Angela and Tracy whom she specifically mentions at the end. Nor is it clear to me that it is solely in virtue of being girls that Angela and Tracy are made fun of. Some research suggests (Willis 1977) that boys who are 'always going on' and 'think they're it' receive similar treatment from their classmates. In some girls' schools, too, the pupil culture of 'cool' which does not permit enthusiastic engagement in school life, makes for some very difficult negotiations on the part of those girls who are interested in working and yet who do not want to be identified as 'teachers' pets' or 'crawlers'. Issues of culture, social class (McDonald 1980) and questions concerning what ability means in this society are also important. However, in spite of these complexities what is worrying about this girl's comment is that it makes reference to the notion of girls 'asking for it'. I wonder whether any boy, however much he was perceived to be an 'earole', 'swot' or 'brain-box' and however much he was 'teased' by his peers (a euphemism if ever there was one) would be considered to have 'asked for it'.

Girls' perceptions of teachers' strategies for dealing with the potential disruption of boys whenever girls speak were remarkably accurate:

Third-year girl: 'The teachers don't give you a chance even if you do decide to say something. They're too worried about the boys starting to play up so they don't let you say things properly. You don't get time so it all comes out wrong. They let boys work things out and we don't get fidgety. It's not fair, I always feel I have to hurry up'.

What is being denied to girls is the public space to engage in exploratory talk which requires a particular kind of trusted group atmosphere so that ideas can be voiced, tested and retracted. As teachers, we ought in my view to be concerned that girls do not have this space but not surprised if they choose silence as the alternative to the risky business of thinking aloud. Silence in the circumstances, is a sensible response.

It has often been said that girls have a civilizing effect on boys: 'The boys' natural inclinations to "push and shove and barge about" are curbed by their girl co-workers.' (*TES* 1984c.) This role is not unproblematic for girls because their efforts to control the boys often rebound on them:

Second-year girl: 'Some of them are alright but when we're watching the video they make too much noise and we can't say anything to them. If you tell them to shut up they give you the fist and if it looks like we're interested in the programme they think we're trying to be it.'

While many girls seemed to arrive at an awareness of how boys behaved through the process of discussion with other girls or with teachers there were some who were remarkably clear from the outset. These were girls who had known both mixed- and single-sex schooling. A fifth-year girl who had transferred from a girls' school to a co-educational one said:

'When there are boys in the class it makes a difference. It's not only what they say and how they make you feel – like you shouldn't say anything in the lesson but just sort of how they are.'

Int: 'What do you mean?'
Girl: 'Well, they spread out. If you get up for anything their legs are always sticking out and you have to climb over them.'
Int: 'Perhaps they're bigger than girls.'
Girl: 'No it's not that, it's not that – they try and make themselves bigger. They lean back on their chairs and stick their elbows and knees out – they take up room on purpose.'

A sixth-year girl who had transferred from a mixed school to a single-sex sixth form wrote about her perceptions of the differences, and non-verbal behaviour of the kind which has already been revealed figured large in her memory:

The most obvious put-downs in the classroom were always the audible tuts and expressions of impatience when a girl asked a question which had become a fairly rare event by the fifth year. If it was an intelligent question which the teacher was interested in answering then they would grin and nudge each other and giggle nervously as the teacher answered. If it was a silly question on a point which the rest of the class understood then they would laugh derisively until the girl was embarrassed into silence or turn to her and make critical comments after the teacher had replied. When the boys asked questions, everybody would usually wait quietly until they were answered unless it was a particularly stupid question in which case they would giggle a little.

Outside the classroom

Outside the classroom a wide range of non-verbal behaviour directed by boys towards girls was very much in evidence. Sexually appraising looks, many types of threatening gesture, boys holding their noses when girls passed in corridors and pretending to talk about them in a very obvious way, imitating their steps and mock fighting to impress, all had their counterparts in girls avoiding groups of boys if possible, sometimes without realizing they were doing so. Many teachers reported that girls found it difficult to begin any discussion of this because they had come to treat the situation as a normal part of day-to-day life (which it is). Again those girls who had experienced both mixed- and single-sex schooling had no difficulty in analysing life outside the classroom.

Sixth-year girl: 'Yes I do notice the difference being with all girls. If you'd asked me two years ago when I was at A . . . I would have been rather annoyed. I like to see myself as quite strong so I wouldn't have admitted to being affected by the boys – anyway you don't notice it if it's happening all the time.'

Int: 'What would you say now?'

Girl: 'Well there's so much really – it's like being in a different world. You don't have to worry about where you go for a start. At A . . . you would walk another way rather than go past a load of boys. It's the way they look at you, you feel undressed or they make obscene gestures. Sometimes they pretend to be talking about you or they hold their noses. One of them might follow you either imitating your walk or doing a hulk behind you and the others would laugh. Or they just nudge each other as you went by or not even that, just staring at you. You know all the things – like when there's a group of blokes on the pavement and you cross over and walk on the other side.'

Both the boys and the girls claimed to have little to do with each other outside the classroom:

Second-year girl: 'We don't have much to do with the boys at break – they're stupid always showing off and showing how tough they are.'

and

Second-year boy: 'Boys don't hang around with girls – they're boring – they don't do anything.'

But the girls' perceptions of the boys' behaviour was rather different. They did not feel that boys ignored them:

Int: 'Do you agree with the boys when they say they ignore you?'

Third-year girl: 'Yes, well no, well it's difficult – they pretend to – they try to – like we're not worth bothering about but they're always mucking up what we're doing. If a group of us are just having a chat they'll barge right through us.'

Int: 'So do you think they are interested in you?'

Girl: 'Well I can't explain it. They don't treat you like a person in school – it's not like being friends with a girl because we're interested in each other. In school it's like we're nothing but they are always on at us, like we're servants and like they're saying "look how tough we are", they do karate punches and things.'

Int: 'Would a boy on his own do that?'

Girl: 'Not really no, they mostly do all the karate and stuff when there are other boys to impress. G.R. and me live in the same road so we sometimes walk the last bit together. He's like a different person, quite normal then.'

It is not clear from this whether boys gain courage from each other to try to impress girls or whether the girls are merely instrumental in boys displaying their prowess to each other. Girls' comments sometimes support one view and sometimes the other. Boys' comments are consistent in maintaining that girls are not worth bothering with but when presented with the evidence of what girls said it gradually emerged that boys do 'hassle girls' – or rather that 'other boys' do. Again both explanations (to impress girls and to impress other boys) figure in the interviews:

Int: 'You've said that boys do hassle girls, why do you think they do?'

Fourth-year boy (a):   'To make sure they toe the line, so they know who's boss.'

Fourth-year boy (b):   'You're really primitive J . . . You make me sick with all this caveman stuff.'

Boy (a):   'It's not me I'm just saying why they do it.'

Boy (b):   'Yeah and you love it. Anyway it's got nothing to do with that. It's a way of proving that you're one of the lads. You know so-and-so is a right lad, a real man, boys do it to each other, girls are irrelevant.'

What seems to emerge from this is that, contrary to popular myth about the independence of boys, they are in fact highly dependent on others. Yet there seems to be two sorts of dependence at issue. John Stoltenberg (1977) suggests that: 'A man's comfort and well-being are contingent upon the labour and nurture of women, but his identity – his "knowledge of who he is" – can only be conferred and confirmed by other men.' If this is the case, boys' attempts to impress girls are not the same as their attempts to impress other boys. In the one case girls are needed to provide servicing, whereas in the other boys depend on other boys for their identities as men. Shows of strength to other boys are about proving the legitimacy of a claim to be a 'real man', whereas to girls perhaps they indicate the possible use of force if servicing tasks are not performed. The theme of servicing is one which emerged strongly through the material and one to which I return later (p. 50).

While body language, what I have called 'style and gesture', has a life of its own, independent of verbal comments, it also occurs in conjunction with what is said.

Language

A great deal of what is said by boys to girls inside and outside classroom constitutes verbal abuse and in my view a form of sexual harassment. Both sexes reported very little equivalent behaviour from girls to boys which confirms the research quoted earlier (Brina 1981). 'Stupid' is a term which girls use against boys but it seems to refer to behaviour not to academic ability. Comments made by boys seem to fall into two broad categories. The first kind are a form of insult having a non-sexual content, the second contain overt sexual meanings. Inasmuch as both are directed predominantly at girls by boys in a mixed school, both constitute a form of sexual harassment.

The first group of comments is clearly meant to depress girls' achievements: they form a constant attack on girls' intellectual and academic abilities. Along with the sighs and groans when a girl speaks for any length of time many instances were recorded of comments like 'turn it off', 'here it goes', 'pull its plug out' and so on. The way girls were referred to as 'it' was felt by a number of women teachers to be particularly offensive. There was ample evidence to show that girls are aware of what boys will say if they make themselves too visible in lessons:

Fourth-year girl: 'Girls often complain to each other about the assertiveness of the boys during lessons but rarely say anything about it. I think they are afraid of being labelled "butch" or "bod" or "intelligent" or "unfeminine".'

Girls are also careful about revealing their marks to boys, for similar reasons. It is no surprise that boys' comments include both an attack on girls' academic ability and on their femininity since being 'intelligent' is considered to be at odds with displaying appropriate characteristics of femininity:

Sixth-year girl: 'When my friends did well in tests or essays, they would put it down to luck whereas the boys were always immensely pleased with themselves. I was the enigma. I rarely put good marks down to luck and I didn't understand why my friends always did until I had thought about it carefully. The boys always over-reacted to my good marks, rolling about in their seats laughing and calling me "bod" and "boffin". My marks became the class joke and yet when any of the boys did as well or better than me the others reacted with genuine admiration. Because I was fairly intelligent, because I asked articulate questions, because I didn't shrink with embarrassment when the attention of the class was focused on me they de-sexed me in some way. After a time the boys would come to me for help with a maths question or an essay but they would make jokes together in the classroom about me "getting off" with someone or looking pretty as if these were events which were never likely to happen.'

If there are over 200 ways to verbally abuse a woman then most of them appeared in the information gathered. In one report a teacher asked a group of girls to make a list of names they knew boys used about them. After half an hour seventy-two names had been collected. When the activity was repeated with another group over eighty words had been collected and more than half were different from those which had been listed by the first group. In the circumstances, it seems best not to reproduce them as they were sent to me, because they are generally appallingly graphic and foul, creating images of women's bodies that are no less than pornographic. If I ever felt tempted towards the unpardonable sin of reacting in an 'aggressive' or 'extreme' way it is now, as I look at these words. On a number of occasions women teachers have commented on the lists: 'They hate us, this is the language of hate.' Leonard Schein (1977) agrees:

For men to become fully human, to liberate ourselves from forced sex roles, and to fully understand ourselves, one of the first things we must deal with is our hatred of women. We have to understand the origin of our mysogeny and the full significance of the fact that we live in a patriarchal society. Patriarchy's foundation is the oppression of women. The cement of this foundation is the socialization of men to hate women.

But it may be objected, girls use the same words to insult each other: go into any girls' school, the objection continues and the same insults might be heard being hurled by one girl to another. This is both true and false. It is false in claiming that the same words are used for there is nothing that even approximates to the range of abusive language used by boys. However, it is true that girls insult each other with words from the milder end of the continuum. What this shows is not that there is a simple, albeit softer, equivalent state of affairs in which boys sometimes abuse girls and sometimes girls abuse each other, but rather a much more complex situation.

First the language of abuse is by and large female. There are no male equivalents of 'tart', 'scrubber', 'bitch', 'cow' and 'slag' (to mention but a few of the milder epithets). As *the* language of abuse it can be directed at anyone by anyone: in being female it speaks volumes about how women are valued in this society. In this sense when a boy calls another boy 'cunt' he not only insults him but does so in a language which degrades women. When a girl insults another girl by calling her 'slag' she too uses a language which is pejorative of women so that in abusing another girl she also, in being female, degrades herself. Second, boys' and girls' relationships to the language of abuse are very different: both degrade women when they use it and girls degrade themselves in a way that boys do not.

A number of girls expressed the belief that particular forms of abuse are restricted to certain groups of boys. A black girl writes: 'They offend you through abuse strictly used by black boys and in slang, using words like "crusty", "fusty", "tight" and "fit" that will not only offend you but put you to shame.' (*Spare Rib* 1983.) Yet the information gathered shows first, that the same words are common currency among white boys and that there is also a tendency for white girls to believe (falsely) that such forms of abuse are peculiar to white boys. Thus, from the evidence available, I would suggest that 1 no particular group of boys indulges any more or any less in this behaviour than any other, and that 2 girls falsely tend to locate the problem as stemming from boys in their own racial, cultural or social class group.

Other comments were recorded which, without overt abuse being used, also made girls self-conscious of their sexuality and of the fact that they were continually being objectified by boys:

Fourth-year girl: 'They don't have to even speak to you for you to know that you're being judged as a sex object. They make comments about other girls' bodies, they talk loudly about what they've done so as you can hear, they compare girls in their hearing and worst of all they discuss how great this video is or that one. Just yesterday I told F.H. to shut his filthy mouth when he was describing how this bloke in this video stubbed out his cigarette on a woman's breast. It doesn't do any good they just do it more if they know you're affected.'

And: 'continual talking about periods, asking whether you were on or not or wearing a Dr. White etc. . .' (*Spare Rib* 1983).

I am not claiming that all boys engage in this behaviour or that what has been revealed so far is a total description of relationships between boys and girls in school, but rather that for every girl in a mixed-sex school it forms a significant part of her experience, either directly or indirectly. As well as all this there is also pupil solidarity. One girl already quoted who was very critical of boys' behaviour was also busy at the time of interview organizing a petition on behalf of a boy who had been threatened (unfairly she thought) with suspension.

Not all boys abused girls; some were described by the girls as 'quite civilized'. A number of boys thought that 'what girls have to put up with is bad' and this led them to the conclusion that 'I'm glad I'm not a girl.' This tends to suggest that there was an assumption of inevitability in operation. One boy did not agree:

Fourth-year boy: 'Of course it's not natural, it's part and parcel of the way men try to dominate women in this society. I don't think it's any great shakes being male, sometimes it's an embarrassment.'

A few boys were similarly critical of the ways other boys behaved towards girls but said they would have a hard time 'going public' on it. One case emerged of a third year boy in a single-sex school who had actively challenged a male teacher's sexism. The teacher had suddenly announced to the class: 'Quick lads there's a naked woman running across the playground.' All the boys with the exception of S . . . leapt up and rushed to the window. Then he said: 'Alright you can sit down now, I was just checking you were normal.' S . . . said: 'I think that's sexist sir.' A number of obscene comments were made amidst a general atmosphere of derision. The teacher made no attempt to quell the noise and when quiet had returned to the class he commented: 'Thank you S . . . now we know who isn't normal.' After school S . . . was threatened, comments such as 'poof', 'S . . . is a woman' and worse were shouted and as he got on his bike a pump was repeatedly jabbed into his rear. He said that after this he kept a low profile in class because whatever he said, even in reply to a question about verb tense, brought forth sniggers from the other boys. Many features of this incident are similar to those experienced by girls and he reacted similarly, with silence.

Physical molestation

Examples of sexual harassment do not stop at verbal insult. The following situations can be viewed as themes rather than isolated incidents:

boys grabbing girls' breasts, dropping things down their blouses and pinging their bra straps, looking and slipping their hands up girls' skirts and boys exposing themselves. More subtle forms of 'touching up' were reported as having been done under the guise of boys looking at girls' work and getting closer than was necessary when lining up or when class organization was other than in rows of ordered desks. Less subtly, boys' preoccupation with girls' changing rooms and toilets seem to take on another dimension. As well as the fact that boys try to get into these areas of girls' space a disturbing amount of graffiti appears. In one school it was reported that tomato ketchup had been poured round the toilet seats the significance of which seems particularly horrible.

Many examples confirm as commonplace these already published reports: 'In science lessons we had to sit on stools with holes in the actual seat. . . . The boys used the holes to stick rulers, pencils etc. up them, when the girls were sitting on them.' (*Spare Rib* 1983.) And:

T.B. was sitting next to me and he kept putting his hand up my skirt. I told him to stop, he didn't and finally I slapped him round the face. The male teacher said something to the effect 'that's it Ros don't let him get away with anything'. It was accepted as a joke as though he was a right lad for trying it on. I was showing a little bit of hesitance like a girl should. (ibid.)

What is unusual about this case is that the teacher was aware of the entire scenario (though his response was indefensible). Many girls complained that teachers, oblivious to the reasons for a girl's apparently 'unprovoked' attack on a boy, would then punish her and accuse her of being 'anti-social'.

In the corridors and other spaces outside the classroom the situation is worse. Some girls in newly amalgamated schools resented the policy of being let out of school ten minutes before the boys to allow them time to get clear of the building. They complained that they were being deprived of lesson time through no fault of their own. Others with a more cynical attitude to schooling made comments like:

I don't care if I lose school time, it's the principle of the thing I object to. If this work is supposed to be worth doing then we're missing out. Anyway did you hear about that second year? She was sexually assaulted by six boys last week and that was at break – how are they going to stop that, lock us up?

Many single-sex schools amalgamate for sixth-form work. Often girls, mostly those doing science and maths, have to go to the boys' school for their lessons. As a way of avoiding harassment girls were advised to maintain a seclusion in their common room for as long as possible:

At the very beginning of our course we were constantly having our bums pinched and more annoyingly held, calmly and with no hesitation whatsoever. We reported this and it was suggested that we wait for five minutes after the beginning of lessons before moving from the common room and leave a couple of minutes early. This meant us missing between five and ten minutes of our lessons.

But corridors and stairways cannot always be avoided; girls do have to change lessons and move between sites:

There was one event last year which sticks out in my mind. Two of us were leaving the boys' school by an outside stairway at the beginning of lunch time. We were walking along talking when a couple of boys aged about fourteen began edging towards us. One passed unnecessarily close and growled to his mate, 'Cor I'd like to squeeze her tits'. Amazed, we turned to the boy and told him how disgusting his attitude was. How dare we speak to him like that! . . . 'obviously slags, slags, slags, slags.' He continued to shout loudly at us as we continued out of the school.

One of the things which shocked many women teachers who spoke to girls is the extent to which they, initially at least, regard sexual harassment as a normal part of daily life. Perhaps this is because 'Intimate violation of women by men is sufficiently pervasive in . . . society as to be nearly invisible.' (McKinnon 1979.) Even in the junior school, those who should know better appear to have little by way of respect or sensitivity towards girls. Commenting on the impact of computers in school one HMI said at a conference:

Children get to school before eight in the morning and don't go home until the caretaker throws them out. It's marvellous. . . . The ribs of the girls are bruised by the boys because they are being pushed out of the way in the rush. In one school special girls' nights are being held to compensate for this. (*TES* 1983b.)

This statement is in my view quite outrageous and beyond comment. Note also that what would seem to amount to any access at all to computers for girls is described as 'special'. Next we may expect to hear the familiar cry 'But what about something special for the boys.'

Some girls were very clear that sexual harassment in the co-educational secondary school was not a new phenomenon in their lives:

At the time I never regarded sexual harassment as a really major problem. It was more like a game which had developed from the infant and junior school with 'kiss-chase' and boys pulling up your skirt. . . . I only really began to get annoyed when it became more than a joke and started to happen all the time. I suppose the embarrassment annoyed me more than the act itself. If you're seen with boys continually chasing you etc. then you get a reputation for 'liking it'.

One strategy that women have always used is to laugh off such incidents. This is because there is always a dilemma about whether any challenge will result in even more humiliation. However, such events are never a joke even though we may have learnt that it is safer to treat them as such. That girls learn so young that violation of their person is a game says a great deal about the extent to which it is a 'normal' feature of women's lives. Sexism (to put it mildly) is no more of a joke than any other form of oppression. But while few in education would dare to openly take issue with say, an anti-racist stance, many deny that there is anything inhumane about sexism. This testifies to little more than either a gross or a deliberate failure of imagination as well as denying the experiences of black girls.

Servicing

Boys' behaviour towards girls not only controls them but is also used to extract an enormous amount of servicing from them. In class girls provide boys with an endless supply of pens, pencils, rubbers and other equipment. Outside the classroom there is a further extension of it:

Recent female school leaver: 'At break times the gap was even more evident . . . the girls sat on the benches in the playground and the boys played football in the winter and tennis in the summer. The girls would go out to the shops with lists of the sweets and crisps required by the boys who would also hang around begging sandwiches. I found the way that the girls in the top set mothered the boys quite incredible: they helped with homework and excuses and even sorted out arguments and disputes.'

The next writer is very clear in her explanation:

The black girls in this school have to just play along with the boys. For example they cling on to their arms making them feel 'nice' and 'outstanding' as they walk down the corridors. They 'lend' them money to buy food and 'fags' or even do their homework for them. The black boys don't even have to say please, they just spell out what they want in plain and sometimes unmanly language with a hint of a smile and why do we black girls put up with it? Well again everybody wants to have a good name, image and reputation by everyone and if this can be gained from a black boy your troubles are over. (*Spare Rib* 1983.)

It would be pertinent at this point to know how many readers have assumed that the comments before this last one were made by white pupils and whether, because the last quote specifically mentions black boys, any different response was initiated. At the same time as discussing this we might take issue with those involved in 'multi-cultural education' who spend hours debating which is worse, racism or sexism. Instead, we might concentrate on who benefits from such abstract and academic debates? Who gains from the competition? Certainly not black women whose lives are not changed in any way by such speculation and who are often rendered invisible by assumptions that 'all the women are white and all the blacks are men' (Hull, Scott and Smith 1982). Even the separation of racism and sexism is for black women sometimes unhelpful:

We know that there is such a thing as racial-sexual oppression which is neither solely racial not solely sexual, e.g. the history of rape of Black women by white men as a weapon of political repression. (Moraga and Anzaldua 1981.)

However, in other contexts such separation is clearly necessary: 'We struggle together with Black men against racism, while we also struggle with Black men about sexism.' (ibid.) It stands as further evidence of the racism and sexism of British schooling that while many have heard of William Wilberforce, few know of Sojourner Truth. As one who simultaneously experienced race and sex oppression she represented in her presence and her speeches her position as a black woman without the right to vote over a century ago:

That man over there says that women need to be helped into carriages and lifted over ditches and to have the best place everywhere. Nobody ever helps me into carriages or over mud puddles or gives me any best place. And ain't I a woman? Look at me! Look at my arms! I have ploughed and planted and gathered into barns and no man could head me. And ain't I a woman? I could work as much and eat as much as any man – when I could get it – and bear the lash as well! And ain't I a woman? I have borne thirteen children and seen most of them all sold off to slavery and when I cried out with my mothers grief, none but Jesus heard me! And ain't I a woman? (Hooks 1981.)

While it would be wrong to assume that all issues are the same for all women (for example, while white women may campaign for the right to abortion, for black women or women of colour the issue is often enforced sterilization or contraception (Roberts 1981)), it is equally mistaken to assume that what has been described so far as the experience of girls in co-educational schools is the experience of white girls alone. Neither is it the case that any one racial group of boys is in the lead in harassing girls. It is necessary to emphasize this point, since on a number of occasions in workshops on this material a disproportionate amount of interest had been shown in the behaviour of black boys and the welfare of white girls. All girls are vulnerable and all entitled to equal concern.

The individual and the group

So far, in presenting the material gathered, I have perhaps given the impression that what is at issue is simply a case of an individual girl being silenced by an individual boy or group of boys. The effect however is wider than this. Whichever individual boy is involved in what one commentator described as 'being beastly', he does not just gain greater space for himself but for all boys. This is because not just one girl is humiliated into silence, for example, but rather all girls in being girls are equally vulnerable to similar treatment. His gain is not just her loss: her humiliation affects all girls and benefits all boys. Perhaps this is why girls 'get edgy' when one of them is talkative in class. She breaks the rules not just for herself but for all girls. The effect of this is that in a class of thirty pupils fifteen are eliminated from the competition for teacher attention and other resources. Perhaps it also sheds light on recent complaints about single-sex groupings in mixed-sex schools: '. . . the sheer scale of discipline required to teach thirty-three second year boys.' (*TES* 1984c). Furthermore, boys who do not display sufficient evidence of masculinity, or more rarely those who actively challenge the sexist behaviour of other boys, are prime targets for a good deal of what is called in their case 'bullying'. Therefore it is doubly in their interest to adopt dominant patterns of male behaviour or at least to pretend to. The question here is when does the pretence become so like the real thing that it is the real thing. The point is in any case that all boys benefit from the 'ethos of male' whether they want to or not.

In my view it is indisputable that boys benefit from their behaviour towards girls: we have seen how and why they are serviced by girls, how their access to educational resources is maintained and how they are active in structuring relationships of dominance and subordination. In this sense we begin to see that there is a political dimension to co-education: that of men's power over women.

3 Natural predators?: yet another critique of biological explanations

Before moving on to explore the political dimension of co-education one other explanation for the difference in behaviour of boys and girls has already emerged: the head of science in wondering whether 'it's biological or something' was merely more explicit than many. That biology explains or causes differences in gender is a pervasive notion in education. Katherine Clarricoates (1980) reports this comment made by a male junior school teacher: 'I think boys tend to be a little more aggressive and on thinking about it the male is the same in the animal world. We are animals basically.'

Comments made in the process of this study carried similar explicit assumptions concerning the causal role of biology – 'there might be a hint of biology in all this, different hormones and things', or 'women give birth after all'. But mostly assumptions about biological determinism were implicit – 'boys will be boys' or 'well they're boys aren't they?' Again many of the proposed strategies, in placing the onus entirely on the girls to find ways to 'cope with the attitudes of the boys' (*TES* 1984c), seems to assume that such attitudes and behaviour are in some way an unchangeable fact. In the light of all this it is time to assess the assumption that a difference in biology explains, because it causes, a difference in behaviour.[1]

To discover that human beings can be divided into two groups, one has only to visit a nudist beach. Biological sex, it would appear, can be attributed quite straightforwardly on the basis of what we see in a person's physical appearance. Even those with a more scientific orientation to life than most of us, like doctors, have no difficulty in asserting with confidence that the baby just born is either female or male.

However, in reality the matter is a little more complicated. Biological sex can apparently be ascertained accurately only by analysis of chromosome structure – the primary sex characteristics. The secondary sex characteristics – absence or presence of body hair, possession or otherwise of breasts, uterus, clitoris and so on – have more to do with the presence or absence of certain hormones (Raymond 1980). Thus anomalies can arise – persons thought to be women can turn out to be chromosomal men and this may be discovered by 'girls' turning into boys at puberty or by 'women' seeking to discover reasons for their infertility after marriage ('Horizon', BBC2 1979).

Furthermore, it seems that the very criteria which we may use on the nudist beach turn out to be culture specific:

Again the degree of difference between male and female somatypes varies between ethnic groups. In one small-scale ('primitive') society for which there are good photographic records – the Manus of the Admiralty Islands – there is apparently no difference at all in somatype between males and females as children, and as adults both men and women tend to the same degrees of mesomorphy (broad shoulders and chest, heavily muscled limbs, little sub-cutaneous fat) which is not found to the same extent in American and Western European groups. In Bali, too, males and females lack the sort of differen-tiation that is a visible sex difference in our culture. Geoffrey Gorer once described them as a 'hermaphroditic' people; they have little sex differential in height and both sexes have broad shoulders and narrow hips. They do not run to curves and muscles, to body hair or to breasts of any size. (Gorer remarked that you could not tell male and female apart, even from the front.) Another source informs us that babies suck their fathers' breasts as well as their mothers'. (Oakley 1972, p. 30.)

The implication of this is that our claim to know that someone is female or male can be problematic. However, the demands of academic rigour aside, few of us would think it necessary in our day to day existence to include with our lesson plans for the day a chromosome testing kit before being prepared to ascribe biological sex to boys and girls. The criteria we use may not be perfect, but by and large we get by with them. Our concepts of gender, and more specifically the models we use in explaining gender difference, are quite another matter. Before mov-ing on to discuss how adequate (or inadequate) the biological model is in explaining the difference in behaviour between males and females, it is necessary to give a rough definition of what is meant by gender and to sketch those differences that are being referred to by the term 'gender differences'.

By gender, I mean those characteristics of behaviour or personality said to be true of, or appropriate to, a person's biological sex or, more 'scientifically', the 'norms of masculinity and femininity' (Terman and Miles 1936). On a common-sense level it is easy to list the gender differences between boys and girls: associated with masculinity are traits like dominance, aggression, strength, objectivity, decisiveness and so on; we would, on the other hand, expect characteristics such as nurturance, dependence, weakness and submissiveness to be given as features of femininity. However, this whole area is fraught with difficulty, and this can be illustrated by mentioning just two difficulties which arise for women. First, although strong and pervasive assumptions about gender do operate in social life (we have specific words for children whose biological sex is not convergent with their gender – 'tomboy' and 'cissy'), these assumptions are in fact totally incoherent. There is no way, for example, as Sue Sharpe (1976) has pointed out, that one can actually be a woman if what that means is to be adult and feminine. This is because to be adult (e.g. independent) and to be feminine (e.g. dependent) stand in direct contradication. Second, in the case of women it seems that we could compose at least two lists which would apparently contradict each other in the terms of the kind of value judgement being made. The first might begin something like this: vain and self-absorbed, manipulative, purveyors of gossip, unable to concentrate; and the second like this: other directed, supportive, co-operative, patient, devoted. On closer inspection, it turns out that the second is an account of how women ought to be and the first a description which not only discloses how we 'really' are but often justifies our inferior social position.

Having made a distinction between biological sex (and here a further distinction between primary and secondary characteristics) and gender, which has more to do with actual or expected behaviour, I shall move on now to the main point, which is to attempt to answer the question How adequate is the biological model in explaining gender differences (differences in behaviour such as we saw in the last chapter) between girls and boys?

The biological model

The assumption that it is biology which determines gender remains a pervasive if not altogether popular notion. The reason why it is not popular with some people is that if men are biologically determined to be dominant and aggressive and women to be 'submissive and weak' then the struggle to change women's position in society or girls' position in school is a waste of time ('But you can't change human nature'). How the biological model explains the existence of strong women who are clearly not 'submisssive and weak', like many whose comments appeared in the last chapter, remains something of a mystery. As El Saadawi (1980) says: 'However, to be contradictory is the essence of all logic based on exploitation.' The postcard (below) neatly reveals that contradiction:

Despite these contradictions, the biological explanation remains a pervasive one: as we have seen, educationalists constantly refer either explicitly or implicitly to a biological 'something we know not what' to account for the fact that boys are as they are. The fact that it is sometimes unclear what sense of 'biological' is meant and that sometimes it is clear that there are several senses of 'biological' in play (Janice Raymond cites six), presents us with something of a nightmare. There are, however, some recurring themes: that hormones affect gender, that chromosomes do, or that the function/construction of our biological bits do. I shall take the first two together.

Much of the evidence (e.g. the work of the socio-biologists (Wilson 1975)) that aggressive male behaviour is biologically based and that it arises from hormone/chromosomal structure is based on animals, particularly other primates. However, this is not a promising beginning for, as teachers have known for a long time, whatever the biological similarities between rats and children, there are very great differences. Children are born into a social world where the environment is structured through language and symbols and as far as we can tell rats are not. The argument is *not* that 'nurture not nature' is the determining factor in the moulding of gender difference, merely that in using animals to support their biological claims, scientists are not comparing like with like. For example, the fact that women may share with other female mammals the necessary equipment to breast-feed their young does not mean that they necessarily choose to do so; neither is it clear that there is any ape equivalent of *Playboy* in which breasts have other fetishized meanings. Therefore the animal world does not provide us with good evidence. But even if it did, it would seem that the evidence has been carefully selected. Numerous counter examples can be found of male and female animal behaviour that contradicts human gender stereotypes (Fisher 1979), and in one study by Rose a rather startling conclusion was reached:

Female rhesus monkeys infected with androgen show an increase in the 'male' practice of 'mounting' but only if they are dominant members of their group to begin with, before they are injected. If subordinate females are infected, the incidence of mounting behaviour remains the same. Likewise, when dominant male monkeys who secrete testosterone in excess are placed in a social environment where their dominance is not recognised, they become inferior members of the group and their testosterone output lessens considerably.

Thus it can be seen that the role of sex hormones in generating signals that are relayed to the brain and converted into sexual arousal is clearly outweighed by environmental factors. In the latter example of the male monkeys (to reverse the Freudian adage), it is destiny that determines anatomy, or at least determines hormone levels. (Raymond 1980, p. 54.)

This example is particularly interesting because it demonstrates the very confused nature of the subject. Female mounting is already invested with the same meanings as male mounting and there is an implicit link between this and dominance within the social group. Yet such a link is not explored and we are left wondering what the connection is between sexual behaviour, how that is to be interpreted, the animal's position within the pecking order and its general gender identity.

Thus, in conclusion, it would seem that fascinating though animal behaviour might be and instructive though it is in some circumstances, for the purpose of understanding human behaviour and its determinants, evidence based on animals is not a great deal of help since

1   It is partially selected and so makes false claims about the universal connection between female/male and certain types of behaviour.
2   It is irrelevant because whatever mice, rats and pigeons do when injected with hormones does not imply that even if humans engaged in 'similar' behaviour, we could infer the existence of hormones as causal agents. Perhaps, as Rose suggested, it is the other way round.
3   The comparison is not legitimate since human behaviour is learned and acted out in a symbolic, social setting (Jackson 1978).

Perhaps the next step could be to compare humans with humans. However, to understand this as a task in which individuals were compared with other individuals within the same society would be fruitless. However many individuals were compared with other individuals and however many correlations discovered between hormone levels and certain sorts of behaviour, several problems would arise. First, no behaviour comes labelled with appropriate descriptions. Deciding that someone is, for example, aggressive is not done merely on the basis of *what* they do, but also on the basis of *how* they do things. Therefore, we need to be able to give very rigorous criteria for picking out instances of aggression from those of social ineptness or over-enthusiasm, for example, and we cannot do this in any precise way.

All kinds of interpretive categories and assumptions come into play when we describe someone as being aggressive. Second, even if this problem were overcome and a correlation were established between aggression and hormone levels, we could not conclude that the latter was responsible for the former – it might be the other way round. The nature/nurture debate is not resolvable at this micro level because nature and nurture are impossible to separate. Third, it would be even more difficult to explain gender differences between boys and girls using these kinds of procedures because what counts as aggression in girls is very different to that in boys. A girl who swears is often judged to be aggressive in a way that a boy is not (Spender 1982).

What all this demonstrates, I think, is that femininity or masculinity, and the whole range of behaviours which fall into these categories, are not *just* behavioural categories with or without social or biological determinants, but also social, cultural and political categories. Therefore, in order to compare humans we have to look at humans across cultures and not within them. This is a shift of emphasis from the individual and her/his behaviour to the gender system or 'sex role plan' (Sanday 1981).

Margaret Mead is one of many anthropologists who conducted precisely this kind of inquiry. She looked at three very different groups in New Guinea – '. . . the gentle mountain-dwelling Arapesh, the fierce cannibalistic Mundugamor and the graceful head-hunters of Tchambuli' – and found that:

Each of these tribes had, as has every human society, the point of sex difference to use as one theme in the plot of social life, and each of these three peoples has developed that theme differently. In comparing the way in which they have dramatised sex difference, it is possible to gain greater insight into what elements are social constructs. . . . (Mead 1935.)

Among the Arapesh, gender was constructed around our stereotype of femininity – ideal adults were gentle, passive and cherishing. On the contrary she reports the gender identities of both men and women among the Mundugamor approximated more to our notion of the masculine pattern. The women and men were 'assertive' and 'vigorous'. Both sexes detested bearing and rearing children and both sexes were reared to be independent and hostile. In the third group, the Tchambuli, there was a differentiation of gender by sex, but this was reported as the reverse of ours. The men

were skittish, wary of each other, interested in art, in the theatre, in a thousand petty bits of insult and gossip. Hurt feelings are rampant . . . the pettishness of those who feel themselves weak and isolated. The men wear lovely ornaments (the women shave their heads and are unadorned) they do the shopping, they carve and paint and dance. (Mead 1950.)

Of the children she comments:

This is the only society in which I have worked, where little girls of ten and eleven were more alertly intelligent and more enterprising than little boys . . . the minds of small males, teased, pampered, neglected and isolated, had a fitful, fleeting quality, an inability to come to grips with anything. (Mead 1950.)

It is beyond the scope of this chapter to discuss in detail the implications of Mead's evidence for issues such as power, dominance and the alleged universality of patriarchy (Rubin 1975). What it does show is that the biological model is inadequate in explaining gender differences between the sexes.

This is important because often in discussions about education the subordination of girls is justified on the basis of gender characteristics, which are alleged to follow from female biology. All we need to show is that gender identity of human beings varies from culture to culture and the 'natural order' ceases to have quite the degree of necessity which is claimed for it.

But, it might be objected, anthropology is notoriously fraught with difficulties, the relevant one in this case being the problem of interpreting cultures from the outside and within the anthropologists' own categories and framework. Taken to its logical extreme, the sceptical view (that nothing can be said about another culture which is not infected by the values and beliefs of the researcher) ends in a position of absurdity, for nothing can be said about anything which is not 'infected' by a theoretical framework of some sort. This is because even our perceptions of the natural world are mediated by a conceptual framework – to experience at all, as opposed to being the subject of a tide of happenings, is to operate with categories. However, the objection is well put if what it does is to add a cautionary note and it is one which Mead herself might have heeded before using such extremely value laden expressions as 'skittish', 'gossip' and so on.

But if this does not satisfy those disposed to be suspicious of anthropological evidence, now might be the best time to turn to a different sort of evidence: transsexualism. In this case, biological sex and gender go in opposite directions: 'Transsexuals reject the gender that the culture has assigned to them and gravitate toward the gender assigned to the opposite sex.' (Raymond 1980.)

The mere fact that a great deal of money is spent and a great number of people (apparently mostly men) are physically mutilated in the most horrible ways and then kept on damaging drugs for the rest of their lives demonstrates, I think, what is at issue. The maintenance of the gender system as constructed in this society is obviously of crucial importance to someone; more so than the health of its non-conforming casualties. Individual biology (secondary characteristics) can be rebuilt but our notions of masculinity and femininity cannot. Why? Perhaps it is because the social control of women by men can only be maintained if women and men are *constructed* very differently. If we accept that one of the instruments of control of women is male sexuality, *constructed* and predicated as it is on 'objectification, fetishization and conquest' (Snodgrass 1976; *Achilles Heel* 1982), then parameters are drawn within which certain gender identities are appropriate and possible for men and others are not. Similarly, femininity must have its limiting parameters as the reciprocal other half of these. However, if this were the direction in which to seek answers how could the phenomenon of male-to-female transsexualism be accounted for – after all, what I have suggested is that gender is linked with power in the particular way that men exercise it over women in this society. Are male transsexuals to be thought of as men who joined the front line in the struggle against male power? One is not inclined to think so given the often offensive and caricatured notions of femininity which they express (Morris 1974). Various suggestions have been made: Mary Daly sees it as a very new version of a very old idea running through religion of men giving birth to themselves; Janice Raymond (1980) offers this thought:

As female energy, spirit and vitality have not proved conquerable . . . so too has female flesh been difficult to mould and manipulate according to patriarchal standards. Perhaps male flesh will prove more malleable.

This letter from a transsexual confirms her suggestion:

Free from the chains of menstruation and child-bearing, transsexual women are obviously far superior to Gennys in many ways. . . . Genetic women are becoming quite obsolete, which is obvious and the future belongs to transsexual women. We know this and perhaps some of you suspect it. All you have left is your 'ability' to bear children and in a world which will groan to feed 6 billion by the year 2000, that's a negative asset. (Raymond 1980.)

I have argued that not only does transsexualism demonstrate that gender does not follow from biology (seen as chromosomes or hormones), but that it may also give us a clue in understanding gender as central to the politics of patriarchy. I have not attempted to argue this position at this stage, merely to suggest a possible alternative theoretical framework.

I want now to turn to the issue of anatomical sex as determining gender. Shulamith Firestone (1979) has argued that women's oppression is a direct consequence of the fact that we bear children and (less explicitly) that our femininity arises from this and some of the associated features (lactation) of our biological lives. There are several objections to this view, which is one rather popular among teachers. The fact that men and women have different 'reproductive functions' does not automatically demonstrate that power must be unequally distributed between them. This is because if women are rendered dependent while child-bearing, it is not self-evident that this dependency must be on men rather than on other women, or that it must be one man in the form of marriage. Neither is it the case that child-bearing is a continual state for all women or a state at all for some. Third, the argument assumes that men have some innate drive to exploit women's reproductive capacities. The fact that they may do and do exploit us stands in need of explanation and cannot be used as axiomatic. Again, I would want to argue that far from femininity following from child-bearing, the very reverse is true. The construction of femininity (in this society at least) structures child-bearing and links it with child-rearing. If female biology is not helpful in understanding gender difference what of male biology?

While not rejecting the influence of social factors in shaping gender identity ('female psychology') Janet Sayers (1982) argues that (male) biology cannot be totally ignored:

. . . these liberal feminists underestimate the part played by biology, and by sexuality, in shaping psychology. . . . They neglect to mention that the penis also has psychological significance because of its biologically given erogenous character. Neglect of this factor has led such writers (e.g. Thompson 1943) to suppose that in a society that was dominated by women rather than by men breast envy would simply replace penis envy. But in any society, the relative significance given by psychology to the breast and to the penis must be determined . . . among other things by the different degrees to which biology has endowed these different parts of the body with erogenous potential . . . any account of female psychology that neglects the influence on psychology of this latter biological factor will necessarily be an incomplete account of psychology.

There are several problems with this argument. First, the mere fact that the penis has erogenous potential shows little if anything: the clitoris has it too. Is the same potential being used to explain the construction of two very different notions *viz.* masculinity and femininity or are there different potentials? If they are different, how can we know – how can a potential be investigated? If, second, the argument is that the penis has more erogenous potential than the breast, then this may be true or false, but in either case it is irrelevant. Why not on this argument compare the clitoris with the tip of a man's nose. If comparisons are to be made between male and female biological bits then the same items must be compared. Third, if it is claimed that the penis has psychological significance then the question must be raised – for whom? If it has significance for women's psychology then this could only be because men have made it so – because they have power to make what is significant for them, significant for women. The female body has erogenous potential but the public significance of this has been minimal in the past. Fourth, this account makes it impossible to understand why transsexualism should exist at all, let alone on the scale claimed for it because the organ in question is the very one which is removed.

Having argued that the biological model used to explain gender difference is inadequate, I do not think that biology is irrelevant – it is crucial. Without it the gender system in this society would collapse, for it is the only aspect in which men and women differ. In order to create a social division between two groups some actual difference is needed as a legitimating explanatory category. Biology and difference in biology, far from explaining differences in behaviour between boys and girls, is used to give legitimacy to them. Gender differences do not flow naturally from biology but must be seen as rooted in politics. The appeal to biology is merely an excuse and as such must itself be seen as part of the rationalizing ideology of the politics of male domination.

4 Parasite and host: capitalism and patriarchy, which is which?

If the social control of girls by boys is not to be explained by biology but by politics, as I have suggested in the last chapter, then the question arises as to what this might mean. Obviously, what is not meant is that such behaviour is recommended in the Conservative Party's manifesto; numerous though their sins are, this is not one of them. Neither do I mean 'of or affecting the State' (*Concise Oxford Dictionary*). As I shall go on to argue, the social control of women by men is much wider than the parameters of state control. What is meant by 'political' is simply 'involving power'. This is hardly new: there is an entire sociological tradition which looks critically at the role of schooling in reproducing power divisions in society. Sometimes empirical studies have set out to discover whether schooling promotes social mobility (Halsey, Heath and Ridge 1980).[1] Sometimes the work has been more abstract in its attempt to theorize the relationship between social divisions in school and those in the wider society. Bowles and Gintis (1976), for example, point to the ways in which authority relations in school 'mirror' those to be found in the workplace. Although there has been much debate concerning the best way to characterize the relationships between school and the wider society, the central claim has been that schooling is political in so far as it selects and prepares children for their place in society as adults. More specifically, it is argued that school reproduces the social structure, which in our case is capitalism. There is nothing particularly unusual about this: within any society schools are subject to social policy which attempts to ensure that future citizens are imbued with knowledge, values and beliefs necessary to the maintenance of society (Nicholas 1983). In the light of this we may feel less inclined to have much faith in the 'indoctrination/education' dichotomy and although what goes on in Chinese schools tends to be called 'indoctrination' (as opposed to 'education' in the West), when it comes to it we are all involved in the same business: preparing the young to take their places in the future as conforming citizens.

Thus, there is nothing new in the claim that schooling is political if this means that through it the structure of society is reproduced. However, although it is undoubtedly true that in Britain capitalism is reproduced, that is not the end of the matter. Other inequalities are reproduced that are not reducible to the demands of capitalism. Arguments which explain the oppression of women by men in terms of the needs of and benefits to capitalism are, in my view, inadequate. So, too, are theories which explain what girls experience in mixed-sex schools in terms of capitalism. Yet, these are the claims that are predominant in the political critiques of schooling. To be more explicit, Marxist explanations of girls' positions in education are inadequate and, more generally, Marxist explanations or analyses of women's oppression are inadequate. This is because all varieties of Marxism, whatever their internal differences, see the oppression of women as ultimately following from our relationship to the economic system: they see our oppression as following from our connection (or lack of it) with production. Thus, our subordination to men is not theorized in terms of the benefits which accrue to them and the vested interests they have in maintaining those benefits, but in terms of the benefits to capitalism. Zaretsky (1976), for example, in acknowledging that women reproduce the labour force and provide psychological and emotional nurturance for workers amidst a sea of alienation, argues that such activities are required by capitalism and are of benefit to it. Capitalism, Marxists argue, requires the population to be structured into performing certain functions: it needs a private female domestic sphere and a public male sphere – the world of paid work – it needs a stable male labour force and a reserve female labour force which can slot in and out of work at low pay depending on the state of the economy. The point which is never explained is why those divisions have to be sexual divisions or why, within these sexual divisions, women are subordinate to men. Capitalism, to put it crudely, may need someone to scrub the toilet for free so that a worker is kept healthy, but why should that someone be a woman? It was once explained to me that women's noses are less sensitive than men's but this seems to be little more than an extreme case of biological barrel scraping. Heidi Hartmann (1979) states the objection a little less crudely:

Just as capital creates these places indifferent to the individuals who fill them, the categories of Marxist analysis, 'class' 'reserve army of labour', 'wage-laborer', do not explain why particular people fill particular places. They give no clues about why *women* are subordinate to *men* inside and outside the family and why it is not the other way around. Marxist categories, like capital itself, are sex-blind.

Nobody could accuse Heidi Hartmann of academic flamboyance when she concludes: 'Marxist analysis of the woman question has suffered from this basic problem.'

With this in mind, it is perhaps worth returning for a moment to Bowles and Gintis's influential analysis. This can be regarded as typical in arguing that schooling is political in that it embodies structures which function as selective and allocating devices for the social reproduction of the class structure. According to their argument the school produces a differentiated, stratified and conforming workforce, equipped to occupy positions either in the primary labour market (high salaries, career structure etc.) or in the secondary labour market (low job security, low wages, little training etc.). In this secondary labour market are: 'Blacks . . . women, the elderly, youth and *other minority groups*.' (Bowles and Gintis 1976; my emphasis.) Apart from reducing half the population (women) to a 'minority group', Bowles and Gintis offer no explanation of what other selecting devices are operative in ensuring that it is some categories of people and not others who occupy certain places in the hierarchy.

Furthermore, the objection that Marxism fails to explain why women are subordinate to men in the sexual division of labour or why a *sexual* division of labour is necessary at all (why not have some *people* in the private domestic sphere and other *people* in the public world of waged work?), is not the only problem. Male control over women pre-dated capitalism, so how can it be responsible for the oppression of women because, at best, it has made use of an already existing social division, the basis of which remains a mystery. Neither is women's oppression currently confined to capitalist societies: in China the Women's Federation found not only that their liberation was not automatic upon changes in ownership of the means of production and land but also that patriarchal attitudes were particularly resistant to change. As women began to make demands over such issues as marriage, divorce and male violence they found that, in threatening men, their views were very often suppressed on the grounds that they threatened the unity of class interests (Croll 1978). Another problem of Marxism is that by occupying a central role in production, women ought to enjoy greater equality with men. But this is not the case as empirical evidence shows. For example, Haleh Afshar (1981) comments that:

According to traditional Marxist analysis the subjugation of women can be understood in terms of the economic base. Their emancipation will only be possible when women are included in socially productive work and there has been a corresponding rise of economy and culture.

However, her analysis of the position of women in Asiaback, a small village south of Tehran, shows that even when women do become involved in socially productive work (making carpets) there is no corresponding improvement in their position. If anything, it would seem as though women's position has worsened:

Women receive no payment for spinning and weaving. The carpets are sold by men in Saveh where they also buy yarn and dyes. Women have no access to the sphere of circulation and do not own their product nor their means of production. Neither are they able to sell their labour power. Their ability to weave carpets has enslaved them even further in an archaic mode of production which is kept separate from the money economy of the men. (ibid.)

Furthermore, it seems as if women's entry into production, although widening the range of activities open to them (or forced on them), may actually increase the extent to which they are tightly structured under the control of men (Deere and de Leal 1981).

In the light of all this it seems reasonable to make a plea at this point for a theory of patriarchy, rather than a theory of social class, to account for the oppression of women by men and the oppression of girls by boys in school. It will not do for this theory of patriarchy to be understood as 'ideology' as some writers have suggested:

The sexual division of labour involves a close relationship between the ideological system and concrete form revealed in the predominant beliefs concerning the role of women. . . . Ideologies are socially constructed 'systems of representations' comprised of images, ideas and concepts. (Wolpe 1977.)

This is because patriarchy involves more than sets of ideas: rape, male violence and sexual harassment are all very material ways in which men control women. But this could be conceded, ideology it could be claimed is material and hence the Marxist bacon is saved.

This, however, is not a satisfactory explanation because it does not explain the material base of ideology. It is no help to point us back in the direction of the economic base since ideology has already been wheeled in to cover the gap left by the explanation which gives analytic primacy to economic determinants. Thus, the account is circular. Ideology is introduced to explain patriarchal relations because crude Marxism cannot explain why capitalism needs men to dominate women rather than the other way round, yet when we look for the material base of patriarchal relations we are referred back to the mode of production. But, then, if patriarchal relations are material why call them ideological? Only, I suggest, because Marxists need to retain the analytic primacy of economics (mode of production) as the determining factor of other material practices. However, once it is acknowledged that there is not necessarily any connection between patriarchy and particular kinds of economic systems, a new material base for patriarchy has to be found.

Thus, with a sense of relief we may be forgiven for feeling excited that at last an analysis of girls' education is about to sock the sex-blind sociological world squarely on the jaw. Educational analysis is incomplete without an understanding of patriarchy which is, says Madelaine MacDonald (1981), 'A set of social relations with a material base and in which there are hierarchical relations between men and solidarity among them – which enable them to control women.'

However, there is disappointment in store. Just as Heidi Hartmann criticized Marxism for its concentration on the sphere of production, but saw the solution to the problem in terms of understanding male control of women's *labour power*, so MacDonald sees patriarchal relations as being maintained in the interests of the sexual division of labour which benefits capitalism. This theory is inadequate. Why should men, particularly working-class men, engage in practices which subordinate women for capitalism? Men do so because they benefit from it, a fact omitted from both the definition and the analysis. Therefore, although MacDonald's work represents an advance because it considers girls at all and because it details certain aspects of schooling as expressive and reproductive of patriarchal relations, in the last analysis it is inadequate in stating that the material base of patriarchy is in the last instance reducible to the economic and in its claim that patriarchy is maintained solely in the interests of capitalism. As Marxists, Hartmann and Mac-Donald have to give analytic primacy to the mode of production as ultimately determining social relations, but in doing so they never explain why *men* control *women*. What then is the material base of patriarchy – how do men control women?

They do so through their control of women's access to production, and by their control over biological reproduction, but this is not sufficient. A crucial third element which has been omitted from the Marxist account is male control of women's sexuality through a particular form of heterosexuality. The construction of male identity and in particular the social construction of male sexuality is crucial in the maintenance of male power and it is this which we have witnessed in the mixed-sex classroom. I am not arguing that men's control over production or biological reproduction can be reduced to their control over women through the exercise of male sexuality. In practice there seems to be a highly complicated matrix of these three in operation. For example, women's economic position is controlled by sexual harassment at work (McKinnon 1979), but on the other hand the extent to which women are vulnerable to harassment on the street depends on whether we can afford to own cars. Again, our control over biological reproduction is greater or less depending on our economic position; abortions can still be bought and contraception and sterilization without a woman's knowledge or consent are features of white working-class and black women's lives (Roberts 1981). On the other hand, the organization of biological reproduction in this society, with the assumed connection between child-bearing and child-rearing, affects women's access to paid work. The connection between male sexuality and reproduction can also be seen to be operating both ways. The way male sexuality is organized in terms of a model of 'normal' heterosexuality involving frequent coitus makes women vulnerable to pregnancy, especially if they are aware of the damaging effects of many forms of contraception. This model, however, is not universal. Heider (1976) described the Dani of Indonesia as having a low level of sexual interest. After child-birth there is no sexual intercourse for between four and six years. Boys' initiation ceremonies do not emphasize masculinity as we know it and within the society as a whole there is a low level of sexual stimulation as compared with our own sex obsessed culture. On the other hand, in Western society having children pressures women into continued relationships where they are vulnerable to a male sexuality constructed against the interests of women. This pressure (exemplified in the treatment of lesbian mothers) is made explicit by proposals to give fathers rights of access to their children irrespective of the circumstances in which they were conceived, such as rape (Sutton & Friedman 1982). What is striking about the oppression of women by men is that women are pressured into individual relationships with their oppressors. As such the power relations involved are masked by the ideology and language of love, romance, pleasure and desire. This is not to deny that women love men: the structuring of the 'boy meets girl' scenario creates feelings which are real. The point is not to deny that such feelings exist but to point out that they mask the fact that there is a power dimension to such relationships. I have already argued that the explanation for the differences in masculinity and femininity lies not with biology but with politics. It is now time to explain this view. I shall argue that it is the social construction of masculinity or social maleness, central to which is the construction of a particular form of male sexuality, which contributes to the continued oppression of women to the material benefit of men and that this way of looking at things helps us to understand mixed-sex classrooms.

Ethel Spector Person (1980), an American psychoanalyst, has suggested that an obsessive sexuality is central to male identity. Men, she argues, feel driven to 'act out sexually' because that is how they assure themselves of their identity as men. There are some common assumptions about male sexuality. There is the assumption that men have a high sex drive and that this is biologically based, so that if frequent coitus with women is not achieved then they will suffer discomfort or physical damage.[2] This assumed biological need is often used to excuse men from their sexual abuse of daughters and to blame women in the family for failing in their duty of sexually servicing their husbands. Sometimes this biological imperative erupts in the form of rape. Uncontrollable urges, in being seen as a natural part of male sexuality, also function to excuse men's behaviour and again attention becomes focused on the 'provocative' behaviour of the rapist's victim. (The fact that men are highly selective when it comes to choosing the time and place to rape seems not to undermine the assumption of uncontrollability.) This then is the conventional wisdom concerning what is normal, healthy and biologically inevitable about male sexuality, assumptions with which we are all familiar and may even have believed.

Feminists, however, have known for at least a hundred years that this is all claptrap. Although writings and campaigns organized around the turn of the century have been 'written off the record', much recent energy has gone into rediscovering earlier feminist struggles and in mapping the way in which particular forms of male sexuality have been promoted as responses to those campaigns by the so-called progressive sexologists (Jeffreys 1984; Jackson 1984). What this means is that the construction of male sexuality as well as being a material force in the oppression of women, also has a history which reveals on investigation the changes which have occurred (Jeffreys 1983).

There is now a vast feminist literature on this subject and it seems that at long last this has persuaded a small number of men to examine for themselves the nature of male sexuality. We are told by John Stoltenberg (1977) that the so-called biological imperative is a lie and by Jack Litewka (1977) that male sexuality is organized around three basic notions:

Objectification: From a very young age, males are taught by everyone to objectify females. They generalize the female, in an almost platonic sense. This generalized woman is a concept, a lump, a thing, an object, a non-individualized category. The female is always 'other'.

Males learn to objectify through a process of 'definition'. We identify, and have identified for us, many female attributes. It starts simply: girls have long hair, wear ribbons on it, have on dresses, and like pink and yellow things. And, of course, they play with dolls. . . . When it's time to learn practical living skills, they sew and bake while we use tools and build. They are easily recognized as different. There's them and there's us. And who'd want to do a silly girl's thing anyhow?

Fixation: Part of male sexual initiation is learning to fixate on portions of the female's anatomy: at first breasts. . . . And in movies, on TV, in advertisements, where else can we look when the camera's eye focuses on breasts? So our eye is trained and we fixate. Emotionally too. We learn that if we do that, we will eventually get pleasure and have fun. And be men. Be seen as male. Be reacted to as male.

Conquest: To conquer is a highly valued skill in our society. We are taught to alter the enemy into nothingness, to convert the bear into a stuffed head and rug, to gain power and rule. Male initiation rites and activities always require trophies (e.g., sports) and the more numerous and advanced your 'awards', the more of a man you are. In sexual matters, the male conquers when he succeeds in reducing the female from a being into a thing. . . . Conquest . . . follows Objectification and Fixation. I mean, after all, what the hell's the sense of objectifying and fixating if you're not going to get off your ass and do a little conquering? And when we do conquer, what is the trophy? In the old days it might have been a lock of hair or a garter strap. A ring can also announce your achievement. But always your own knowledge of what transpired is your reward – being pleased with yourself and being able to say to yourself, 'I am a man.' And if others have knowledge of your conquest, your knowing that they know is as great a reward as any.

In teenage boys it is an exaggerated form of these elements which seems to constitute masculinity. Julian Wood (1982) says that for the boys he worked with

. . . it was clear that learning to inhabit their form of masculinity invariably entailed, to a greater or lesser extent, learning to be sexist: being a bit of a lad and being contemptuous of women just went 'naturally' together. The boys saw all women as existing primarily in and through their physical bodies (face, legs, tits, etc.). There are precedents for this dissecting attitude just about everywhere.

There is also a price to pay for the power gained over women and girls:

Boys . . . are encouraged to measure their masculinity via a woman-hating rapacious sexuality. This pressure to be a sort of Tarzan-cum-Ripper is sedimented into the history of how to be male. Learnt as a style it may harden into a cramped emotional range which cannot be softened. (ibid.)

These accounts make perfect sense of what we have witnessed in mixed-sex schools. The objectification of girls is both exemplified and achieved by sexually appraising looks, by the reference to them as 'it' and by physical forms of sexual harassment, to mention but a few examples from Chapter 2. Evidence of fixation, what is sometimes called in the literature 'fetishization', appears in the way that particular parts of girls' anatomy become the focus of boys' attention – breasts, legs, buttocks – and in the way that the language of abuse includes a large number of obscene references to particular parts of girls' bodies. Conquest is rather more complicated: girls, like women throughout history, have numerous strategies of resistance and to this extent are not passive victims of boys' behaviour. Often though, such resistance, particularly if it is overt, merely means that boys redouble their efforts (remember the girl who told 'F. H. to shut his filthy mouth' and then went on to say 'It doesn't do any good, they just do it more'). Thus, there is a dilemma for girls: they either overtly challenge boys or ignore them as a way of refusing to participate at all. If boys are aiming at conquest it is difficult to know whether they have succeeded when girls become silent or whether, in mentally switching off, girls do in fact achieve their removal from the arena. Much depends on how far girls are conscious of what is happening, how far they identify as a group and how far opting out is a self-chosen strategy – a refusal to be controlled as opposed to an individual response following the internalization of low self-esteem.

Conquest is not an all-or-nothing business. Women are involved in a continual set of negotiations: go along with it in this instance, object on that one (and know that self-preservation is a tricky business!). This means that a girl might continue to service a boy in class but refuse any further relationship:

Fifth-year girl: 'I told him, I don't want to see you any more. You're really nice when we're together and you're a pig when you're with your friends. He still comes to me for pens and stuff though.'
Int: 'Do you give them to him?'
Girl: 'Yes usually, it seems petty not to. Anyway I don't want outright hostility.'

A great deal more could be said about the construction of social maleness in this society and its use as an instrument in the social control of women, affecting where we go, how we behave, what we do and when (for a much fuller discussion see Coveney *et al*. 1984). However, for the purposes of this study enough has been said to suggest ways in which we might begin to understand mixed-sex schools. The 'problem' is not girls or 'the system' or capitalism but what I have called, for want of a better expression, 'social maleness'.[3]

A central part of the social growth of boys into men involves the social control of girls and women and as such boys' behaviour towards girls does not just reflect an imbalance of power between men and women but actively reconstitutes it.[4] We have seen how girls may choose one boy to 'protect' them from the rest and how individual boys who do not support social maleness are punished along with girls who become too obvious in refusing to accept their place. As such, co-educational schools are one site among many where an identity of maleness is learned, practised and endorsed. Central to this is a particular form of male sexuality which, I have suggested, constitutes one material base of women's oppression. It is now time to consider the implications of all this for equal opportunities work and anti-sexist teaching.

5 Hoeing and humming: possibilities for change*

A great deal of work on equal opportunities and anti-sexism has already been done both inside and outside school. Women teachers (for there are lamentably few men) have worked exhaustively in re-writing materials, making videos and restructuring ways of teaching so that girls have more space in schools. It is now not difficult to gather together lists of contacts and places where further information can be gained about the sorts of initiatives underway (Whyld 1983; WEDG 1983a). There are also groups of women outside schools who campaign against rape, pornography, violence against women, media images of women, sexual abuse of girls, sexual harassment at work and so on. Attempts have often been made to silence what amounts to a feminist fight-back (Wilson 1983). At the forefront of this counter-movement are the usual accusations of totalitarian censorship and prudery. Carol Jones (1984) speaks for many of us when she says:

By focussing only on 'censorship', writers who wish to defend 'video nasties'/ pornography seem to insist on aligning feminists who are critical of male violence on the screen with the increasingly alarming 'right wing' ideology of a Tory Britain (Raynor 1984). I see this as an attempt to silence women who are angry at the butchering of women yet who are also disturbed by the increasing power of the right. It needs to be made clear, here, that feminists campaigning against male violence do not share any political sympathies with the Mary Whitehouse campaign or 'moral majority' (in fact quite the opposite) but that does not mean that we must keep silent about the mutilation of women.

But, despite the fact that a great deal of work has been undertaken on general issues of sexism in schools, much remains to be done with respect to male violence. The first step is to insist that there is a problem

---

* Thanks to Frances McGee for this chapter title.

and this may sound easier than it is. Many people still feel that it is not 'nice' to talk about such things (this is true). Studies such as this one will come under attack for their lack of 'objectivity' without it ever being acknowledged that the so-called standards of objectivity, had they been observed, would not have revealed the information gathered. In my experience it is difficult to raise such matters in mixed-sex groups of student teachers because even when the men are in the minority they can control the conversation with aggression, persistent refusal to treat the discussion seriously or by the accusation that the course is biased because 'it's not a core problem' (Mahony 1983). All of these examples operate as silencers and ways have to be found to negotiate our way through them.

Having established that there is a problem the next step is to understand the full nature of it. This again sounds easier than it is. However, as our understanding grows we will begin to see, for example, the contradiction between, on the one hand, the way we smile fondly as our infant boys 'rough and tumble' in the playground and, on the other, our complaints ten years later about how adept they are at violence. Elizabeth Wilson (1983) quotes this comment in the *Guardian*:

'Boys will be boys' is one of the most insidious phrases in our language and covers a multitude of sins. Boys are brought up to be aggressive and competitive, to 'get into mischief' and generally to behave destructively with only a minimal thwarting of their so-called instinctual drives. In brief, most boys are brought up to be selfish pigs.

Just as we may arrive at new understandings so also we may interpret old knowledge in new ways. For example, if girls choose to work with each other and not with boys in a group we may no longer be surprised. To accuse them of being sexist and to insist, as some teachers do, that they work with the boys is to remove one of the strategies they use to resist male dominance. Neither should we be surprised, as some staff have been, if girls resist attempts to organize them separately from boys. What they resist is the implication that they are the problem in being too weak to be able to cope with the boys (remember the girl who said 'If you'd asked me two years ago I would have been rather annoyed. I like to see myself as quite strong'). This does not mean that we should not organize single-sex groupings in mixed schools but that we should be sensitive about how we do it. At present our sensitivity can be very easily dominated by a concern for the reactions of the boys, which is understandable when attempts to organize women-only groups with student teachers tend to bring forth the wrath of the (male) gods and elicit deep preoccupations with irresponsible spending of tax-payers money which fade abruptly at the rugby club door.

Sensitively managed, however, the provision of single-sex groups in mixed schools can be of enormous benefit to girls, as these comments from the DASI project (Cornbleet and Sanders 1982) show:

Being in the girls' group
Every Tuesday the girls only go to foundation with . . . . and on Mondays with . . . . that is P.E. In the foundation lesson we talk and there is less arguing and less noise and the work I liked was watching the adverts and acting them out and reading books, writing stories and playing games like fruit bowl. The lessons we have with . . . . and . . . . are very noisy and more arguing, and the boys are always calling the girls names or each other.

The work we do is all right but when there's good work I really do enjoy myself. In the girls' lesson I enjoy myself and it is much comfortable and I know the lessons are very good.

Surbjit Kaur
First Year, Clissold Park School

Being in the girls' group
. . . . 's lesson is fantastic. It's really a lesson where it teaches you how to understand girls' feelings, and helps you cope with your problems.

It's a lesson where it's just one sex. Girls: Girls from 1M.

We have one lesson every week which is teaching you about racism and sexism. It's a lesson where you know how girls really feel about sexism, it's a lesson where we're trying to tell you it's just not fair, you haven't got the opportunity boys have, like you get funny names, or should I say horrible names if you ever did design and technology, woodwork, football, because it's known as a boy's subject.

If girls didn't do anything like this, it would be impossible for them to carry on in later life.

All we're trying to do is fight back, fight back for sexism, to get equal with boys. Writing this is very important to me and the teacher because it means really a lot. It's going to be very boring for all of the girls in 1M because we will not be having this lesson next year.

So what I'm trying to say is that I think every mixed school should have this very special and understanding lesson, because if there's any lesson in schools that is important, it's this lesson.

This lesson shows you that you can trust the girls twice more now than you did before. You know how they feel about the whole lesson, because I feel the same.

The world would be wicked if these lessons weren't invented.

Victoria McIntosh
First Year, Clissold Park School

Being in a girls' group

When I first came to this school I expected that everyone, including boys, would be friendly, but after one or two lessons, I realised that boys were just bad and aggressive. Every lesson was the same. The boys were noisy and troublesome and we all got the blame. After a while we started having single sex groups.

I couldn't believe how quiet it was and how much more work we got through without the boys.

The single sex lessons were definitely my favourite foundation lessons.

We learnt a whole lot more about boys and men dominating women and girls. For instance, if a boy has had sex with a girl he is thought of as hard but if a girl has sex with a boy she is thought of as a slag.

Recently there was a D.A.S.I (Developing Anti-Sexist Initiatives) festival. There were many stalls and workshops and self-defence classes and things like that. In the evening there was a brilliant play about being a black girl in a racist and sexist community. It was very good.

I am sad that this project is over.

Rachel Boxall
First Year, Clissold Park School

Despite girls' responses, single-sex groupings have come in for some criticism recently. Sue Jeffery (1984) analyses the opposition:

In a recent report (*TES* 1984c) it was stated that: 'Single sex teaching is not the way to get more girls to take up maths and science, according to the very teachers who have pioneered the so-called "withdrawal" strategy.' The article cites many criticisms made of the single-sex teaching. These boil down to the following points:

1. The strategy is not enough in itself.
2. There can be organisational problems.
3. Teachers do not like it, especially because of discipline problems with all boys groups.

4. Boys do not benefit from the strategy.

5. A lot can be done for girls within the mixed sex classroom.

6. The evidence for the strategy's success is 'confused and difficult to interpret'.

Let us look in more detail at what is actually said in the article and consider how valid these criticisms are.

1 The strategy is not enough in itself because

(a) *The strategy 'could lead to girls getting second-class provision'.*
Possibly true, but this is a failure of the overall school structure and not an indictment of the strategy itself.

(b) *Single-sex groups 'have a limited effect if the school overall remains sexist'.*
True, but this does not mean that the strategy is no good, simply that sexism should be tackled throughout the school. More anti-sexist action is needed, not less.

(c) *Single-sex classes, in isolation, will not attract more girls into physical sciences, and it seems wrong to encourage teachers to think this is all they need to do.*
True, but this is not indictment of the strategy itself. Teachers need to understand that other measures are also necessary.

2 There can be organisational problems because

'Schools can run into the problems of what to do with pupils in the fourth and fifth years, after they have been split lower down the school.'
This is another spurious objection. Why not keep the groups single sex in the fourth and fifth years?

3 Teachers do not like the strategy because

(a) *'Problems can arise within a science department when teachers disagree about the value of segregation, and between the departments when other staff in the school oppose the move.'*
Again this says nothing about the educational value of the strategy itself except that some teachers do not like it (and perhaps may wish to sabotage it).

(b) *'Teachers are often unprepared for "inevitable" problems such as the sheer scale of discipline required to teach 33 second year boys, or the apathy that can be found in an all girls class at times.'*
What exactly is inevitable about apathy in an all-girls class? Is the suggestion that girls are 'naturally' apathetic? Or could it be that teaching materials and methods in science are inappropriate for them? At any rate, the subject should be worth investigation rather than simple assertion and

does not necessarily negate a single-sex teaching strategy. If all-boys classes are harder for teachers to control, this still does not affect the educational value of single-sex teaching for girls.

(c) *A Tameside school achieved 'a remarkable improvement in the girls' scores in the second year science exam' after a single-sex teaching experiment.*

However, we are told rather enigmatically in the article that after some years some staff who had been 'deeply committed' to the scheme had 'turned against it totally'. Why should teachers, who are after all in the business of education, turn totally against a scheme which appears to have 'remarkable' educational success? Again, this situation should be a cause for concern and not simple assertion as if it were an understandable reaction.

(d) The former deputy head of Stamford High School ('This school is the most quoted example of a single-sex success story'), currently on an EOC research grant monitoring the results of mixed versus single-sex teaching, is reluctant to draw 'premature conclusions'. Nevertheless, he admits that girls trail behind the boys in mixed groups. However the 'staff at the school are not "sold on" single-sex teaching, which has raised problems of classroom discipline, and that he quite understands anyone who is suspicious of the technique.' This is a fine example of trivialization, an educationally important initiative when involving girls becomes a 'technique'. Furthermore, why should it be acceptable to be suspicious of initiatives which attempt to remove impediments to girls' learning?

4   Boys do not benefit from the strategy.
Single-sex groups *'do not appear to offer any benefits to boy pupils'.*
Now we are getting down to the real objections – boys don't get anything out of it. The strategy was not designed to offer special benefits to boys. The claim was *not* that boys underachieve in science and maths. The strategy should be judged in terms of the benefits it can offer girls – the original aims.

5   A lot can be done for girls within the mixed-sex classroom.

(a) One teacher claims that both boys and girls benefit from working in mixed sex groups in science. These benefits are: 'The boy's "natural inclinations to push and shove and barge about" are curbed by their girl co-workers and in doing experiments, while the boys rush heedlessly in, the girls concern themselves with correct procedures. Boys learn a lot from girls about setting out their work. You very rarely see a girl leaning over a boy's shoulder to see how to write things up.' The teacher speaking omits to give any examples of how girls benefit from mixed-sex groups, though boys apparently benefit from having mature and responsible pupils (girls) in their class, who service them and curb their 'natural' inclinations. The same teacher declares that girls' participation in physics at the same school has increased, though it appears to be solely due to her example as a female teacher of the subject.

(b) Simple strategies can 'do a lot' to help girls in mixed classes. 'They include asking questions of individual pupils and making sure there is no "girls' ghetto" at the back.' Again the evidence of interaction in mixed-sex classrooms suggests that asking girls questions and pointing them out individually is equivalent to setting them up for ridicule from the boys, since whatever they answer, they will be 'wrong'. Similarly, girls may tend to sit together as a positive way of resisting harassment from the boys. Splitting them up reduces their confidence even further. Even supposing these strategies can 'do a lot' (and where is the evidence for this claim?) can they do as much as single-sex teaching groups? If not, then why settle for them. Do teachers ever refer to 'boys' ghettoes'?

(c) 'It's no use encouraging the girls if they can't cope with the attitude of the boys or if the boys cannot appreciate the ability of the girls in "their" area.'
The assumptions underlying this statement appear to be: it is not worth encouraging the girls as an aim in itself; boys' attitudes are immutable and girls must learn to cope with them; in mixed-sex groups boys appreciate girls' work. But we already know that the last thing that boys do in mixed-sex groups is appreciate girls' work. The attitude of the boys is not questioned or seen as something to be worked on and changed. Again, none of this criticizes the single-sex teaching strategy, except to say that encouraging girls is not in itself a worthy aim!

6   The evidence of the strategy's success for girls is 'confused and difficult to interpret'.

(a) At a Tameside school results in the second year science exam improved dramatically after single-sex teaching for girls:

In 1981, 24% of girls scored less than 50%.
In 1982, 11% of girls scored less than 50%.
Between 1981 and 1982, the proportion of girls scoring over 75% more than
   trebled.

So what is so confusing about these results? Well the 'complicating' factors are:

1   The school changed from being selective to comprehensive. Why should going comprehensive push marks up so drastically? Popular 'wisdom' has it that standards fall when schools go comprehensive.

2   There were several changes in the science staff. This could be a contributing factor, but did boys' results show such dramatic improvements when they were taught by the new staff?

These factors are not so 'complicating' as to suggest that the strategy has failed. If anything they suggest that the experiment should continue to be monitored.

(b)   The second piece of 'confusing' evidence comes from *Stamford High School* where a single-sex experiment in maths began in 1978. Here, the girls taught in mixed-sex groups averaged only 43.9%, while the girls taught in single-sex groups averaged 54.7% in second year. What is so confusing and difficult to interpret about that?

Well, 'the results will not be known' until summer 1985 when a single-sex set has gone right through the school. But the results so far are known and since they demonstrate an improvement for girls then why is this not worth saying?

Sue Jeffery concludes her analysis with this comment:

There is a question as to whether we should exert any energy at all on refuting these very bad arguments, not least because the academic achievement of girls is not the only matter at issue. On balance, I think it is important to analyse in detail and every so often, what is being said. We need to remind ourselves that these are merely some in a very long line of spurious objections to girls being provided with a reasonable context for learning where their primary role is not one of servicing the boys. Isn't it astounding that an article, the whole tenor of which is against single-sex teaching, should produce *no* evidence that the strategy has failed in its original aim which was to tackle the underachievement of girls in maths and science? But the real issue being dealt with is not 'Does the strategy achieve its aim?' but 'Is it worth the trouble?' The answer is 'No, girls' achievement in maths and science is not that important.'

Thus far I have argued that we need to name the problem, understand its nature and origin and be prepared to defend girls' groups from the sort of spurious objections we have just witnessed.

We also need a specific policy on how to deal with the incidents of sexual harassment occurring in school. Carol Jones's (1984) suggestions include:

1. Anti-Sexist initiatives in mixed Comprehensive Schools have included single sex groupings for certain subjects (for example the DASI project) so that girls are able to develop an awareness and confidence together, be in a stronger position to support each other against the boys and create strategies for change.

2. Each school should set up women's groups for teachers, parents and ancillary staff for mutual support, sharing of experiences and discussing action. Girls' groups should be set up and both groups work together on strategies for dealing with sexual harassment. Possibilities include keeping an 'incident book' in which girls/women record sexual assaults. This not only serves to validate girls'/women's experience but may also be useful as 'proof' should the school need convincing. Women/girls should take responsibility for dealing with sexual harassment, to show that women are a powerful force.

3. A room for girls to spend time together is essential so that they do not have to seek refuge in the girls' toilets (many girls do this because it is the only place that is theirs – boys take up the majority of space in the school).

She goes on to add a mild note of caution: 'Men/boys are not likely to take well to these changes and may become abusive to women's/girls' groups. Discretion is, of course, very useful when under this kind of pressure.'

Incidents of sexual harassment do not of course, happen in a vacuum. They occur in the general context of the school ethos and therefore cannot be adequately challenged unless we pay attention to this general context. This requires that we build into the entire curriculum a critical attitude to the presentation of women as sex objects; that we demand that the proper treatment of women becomes a feature of the total school environment. It is not possible to be very specific about what this would entail since institutions differ so much in the ways in which they convey messages about women. For example, in one London college pornographic calendars are a general feature of the maintenance workshops, yet this particular example would not be relevant to schools. However, what would be relevant is the prevalence of 'pin-ups' adorning the insides of boys' lockers and the kind of images of girls and women portrayed in art work displayed around the school (to say nothing of graffiti). So, despite the fact that specific examples differ, there is nevertheless a general question which can be asked: 'What images of and attitudes to women are presented in the general environment of the institution?'

A second question we might ask about the general context of the school concerns language: 'What values about women are embedded in and perpetuated by the language used?' Again this differs from institution to institution. As a Senior Lecturer and in marked contrast to my male colleagues I am variously referred to by male ancillary staff as 'little darling', 'pet', 'love' and 'sweetheart'. In a local junior school on the other hand, the fourth-year girls in asking a male teacher for help with their work are often 'teased' about their subtle attempts to get physically close to him. In both cases the primary concerns of the females in question, whether to fulfil their teaching duties (worker to worker) or to learn (pupil to teacher), are over-ridden by a dynamic of male to female. This dynamic is one in which men patronize women and is all the more difficult to challenge when it arises from friendly, warm, social relationships.

Third, we need to look critically at the written materials used in school. Often this is understood as a task in which we note the absence or invisibility of women, but this is only half the story. Where women are present in texts we must also ask 'How are they portrayed?' 'Is it only as sex objects and in other servicing roles?' A secondary school library could be bursting with books about women and girls but if all the heroines ever do is to swoon while waiting for Prince Charming, then one might argue that this is a kind of visibility that we could well do without.

What might be done about sexist books varies from school to school and depends on resources. One junior school has recently returned 800 library books to the Local Education Authority on the grounds that they were racist and sexist. Another school felt they could not afford to do this as there would be few books left! The staff decided to write critical comments in the texts so that children would see oppressive ideas being challenged. It might be argued that textbooks for use in class should be retained rather than scrapped so the sexist images can be challenged.

Perhaps the most difficult area of all is where children and staff are in social situations. The staff Christmas show is often a glorious example of the superficial way in which anti-sexist work is understood. As a parent, I do not relish the prospect of enduring another evening of 'fun' where various senior male staff caricature 'ugly women' or adorn themselves in all the paraphernalia of sex objectification (suspenders, garters, frilly underwear and the two inevitable over-inflated balloons). While the images of women portrayed are outrageous, these events are very difficult to challenge because the accusation is usually made that one is being humourless and trying to stop people enjoying themselves. In response, it could be pointed out that enjoyment and humour do not necessarily have to be at the expense of others and in any case there is nothing sacrosanct about humour, indeed it is often the only 'legitimate' way that racist and sexist attitudes can be expressed.

Having discussed some general ideas about how we might begin to look afresh at schools, the crucial element which needs to be emphasized is the importance of beginning to talk about the issues. Teachers might begin with small group discussions which range over a number of well-researched issues (option choices, careers, content of school subjects), taking it in turns to provide input based on readings. Consciousness raising groups in which personal experience is a central feature are another valuable way in which awareness of behaviour and strategies for change can be discussed. Small groups of teachers can also make studies of their schools; in uncovering what is really happening in terms of pupil perception, timetabling or examination results, for instance, clear proposals for change can often become immediately obvious. Last, small groups could focus on one issue in school. In the case of sexual harassment, I have argued, there is more which needs to be addressed than the specific instances of harassment.

I have argued that talk generates awareness and that awareness in turn generates its own strategies for change. If this is so, then there is a question about the best way to ensure that talk begins. One way is for Local Education Authorities to insist on it either by imposing policy on schools or by requiring schools to submit policies. Another is to regard the making of policy statements as a secondary issue. The mere existence of these alternatives highlights another issue which is that the role and status of policy and its relationship to practice is highly problematic. On the face of it, it could be argued that when a Local Education Authority starts talking anti-sexist policy, the radical changes are afoot. However the matter is not quite so simple as WEDG (Women in Education Group 1984) point out:

The Inner London Education Authority (ILEA) has a commitment to achieving equality in education and employment within its education service. An Equal Opportunities Unit was set up by the ILEA in order to translate this commitment into practice. One of the main aims of the Unit is to produce separate anti-racist and anti-sexist Statements and Guidelines, for all educational institutions within its domain, which it is hoped will form the background and basis for individual school policies. The anti-racist Statement and Guidelines have been produced and distributed to all educational institutions within the ILEA. Institutions have been instructed to formulate policies in line with them. The anti-sexist Statement and Guidelines are still in the process of being formulated, but will probably act in the same way. In the meantime, however, there are a number of schools that already have policies – how, or whether, they are implemented is, of course, another matter. Those schools that do not already have a policy (probably the majority) may, nevertheless, have individual teachers or a whole staff that is committed to anti-sexist practice and who are developing curricula and strategies for change.

As we see it, there are several problems with the way the ILEA's commitment to 'equality of opportunity' (be it on racial or sexual grounds) is being implemented.

The first problem, and one we have consistently been critical of, is that these 'bits of paper', whatever they are entitled, may well become the end product – where they should only be considered as a concretisation of work already being done, or the first stage in a long and probably difficult process of implementation and commitment. A school's commitment cannot be demonstrated by a policy statement alone. What is more, for those feminist teachers who are constantly in the fore-front of any debate and change, the battle is hard and time-consuming. There should, at the very least, be the time and space provided, within school time for discussion and planning, as well as policy-writing. What is more, without a review or monitoring structure, the policy statement remains static, it requires a continual process of assessment and change.

A second problem with requiring that a policy statement be the starting point for change, means that the initiative is often forced from 'the top', with little, or no commitment from practising teachers. Teachers are required to formulate a policy and then their commitment to it must be won. Obviously this does not always work. For those teachers who are committed to anti-sexist/anti-racist practices, the statement can provide support for, and validation of, their initiatives – these are usually over-worked and under-valued, committed feminist teachers.

Moreover, where anti-sexist/anti-racist work is already being done, a policy statement could be useful in forcing recalcitrant teachers to take the issue seriously and to make changes in their practice (but in the end, changes have to be made in many areas). A piece of paper is not an end product in itself. What worries us most, is that this piece of paper may come to be seen as synonymous with change, rather than the first step in the process of change.

The third problem with the policy statement approach is, without resources of time, money, materials and indeed adequate, committed teachers to try things out – i.e. back-up – the policy statement won't be worth the paper it's written on. Teachers need time to develop anti-sexist/anti-racist curricula and resources. These two areas need careful consideration, so that they are not dealt with as two discrete areas. Otherwise, an anti-sexist policy can become synonymous with 'white girls' and an anti-racist policy synonymous with 'black boys'. We feel it is crucial that these mistakes are not made. Money might be better spent supporting feminist teachers and the development of resources, so that when policies are formulated, there is something to back them up with – both at the level of resources, and at the level of monitoring. Monitoring should, perhaps be done both by the Equal Opportunities Unit and relevant Inspectors and advisors, and by designated teachers/groups within schools. For a 'commitment' to equality of opportunity to be fully realised, those developing policies, at whatever level, must be accountable for the outcomes of such policies. If they do not work, then they must be re-thought and other solutions must be found.

The London Borough of Brent, on the other hand, has tackled the issue rather differently. Hazel Taylor, Equal Opportunities Adviser for Brent, writes (1984);

In Brent I have resisted any pressure that policy should be centrally formulated by me or anyone else in the education department, on the grounds that policy must be produced by the teachers who will implement it if it is to have any meaning for them. If Equal Opportunities is to be taken seriously then it must have implicit in it democratic control of policy making; centralised imposition of policy clearly denies that.

I have also resisted pressure that the Authority should require schools to produce policy quickly because I have been concerned with developing forums for discussion of the issue at more than a superficial level and with the development of practice that actually *works* in terms of changing the life chances of girls (and boys). I was aware of the dangers of policy production being seen as the end without sufficient thought or energy going into how policy is implemented. I also think that on a lot of issues we still don't know what to recommend, but if policy is to be useful it must have guidelines as well. Half-baked new practices are worse than old ones if they achieve notoriety and lose ground for the issue – we need space to experiment to find out what will work so we need plenty of time before anything has to be enshrined in policy.

However after two years in the post I am now recommending that secondary schools be required to produce policy statements because a) some schools have made a lot of progress and the Authority can validate their work by requiring policy which they are ready to develop, based on solid preparation and b) other schools are doing little and won't unless it is required of them. We cannot guarantee that making policy will change practice but we can and must be seen not to let schools ignore the issue. Here the concentration must be on providing appropriate support during the policy making to bring about the maximum effectiveness. I would want to see *all* teachers involved in policy making, with enough feminist teachers spread across departments to ensure that the agenda is properly discussed and sensible recommendations are made. I would much prefer to see a plan of action and review for each school than a policy statement.

This leads me on to the question of monitoring. To be committed to equality, a school must have a series of short and long term aims and actually have conceptualised what a school that does not reproduce patriarchy would look like. It is then essential to decide on time scales for the achievement of change and to monitor progress. If monitoring is not built in there can be no effective evaluation of what is being achieved. In my view, the school should be responsible for monitoring its policy implementation and the Authority should monitor by requiring information on a regular basis about what has been achieved. It is important that this does not become too clinical; some things won't work but teachers will have learnt a lot from trying them, circumstances will vary so much from school to school that priorities will be different and so will speed of action. Also there are very many ways of travelling to the same destination.

This last point raises the question of whether the division between Equal Opportunities and Anti-Sexist education is helpful. In my view it is valuable to be aware that there is a difference in perspective (female access to a male world or changing the world) but to make value judgements about where individuals are at is destructive and uses up energy better spent on dealing with ways of moving people's perspectives. It seems to me that it is necessary to work at all levels with teachers, starting from where they are and moving at a speed they can handle which will be different from individual to individual. That implies that Equal Opportunities initiatives will be right for some people at first. I also think, that while we should not fudge over our real position – which for me involves the necessity of changes in the power structure which at present makes any attempt at equality a joke – we must support people who are changing. Charges of tokenism are unhelpful and so are criticisms of superficiality. A lot of what is labelled tokenist is done in good faith by teachers denied access to discussion or support. I believe it's very important to have as wide support as possible for Equal Opportunities because then there is a more favourable climate of opinion for going further. Attacking Equal Opportunities is a foolish tactic because it feeds stereotyped notions of feminists and loses middle ground support. There are a *lot* of women teachers around whose practice is radical because they are good practitioners but who do not identify as feminists. We need them.

As can be seen from these statements by WEDG and Hazel Taylor there are a large number of issues as yet unresolved and a diversity of opinion between Local Education Authorities and between individuals about the best way to proceed. There is a temptation to feel grateful that the issue of sexism is on the agenda at all, a temptation we would do well to resist when the current initiatives are placed in an historical context.

Moving now beyond the scope of individual schools to more general questions of school organization, it is time to assess whether the information gathered in this study points towards a vote in favour of single-sex education. The answer it seems to me is perhaps, surprisingly, not straightforward (though it has to be said that in the case of my own daughters I had no reservations, all things considered, in opting for a girls' school). While girls in single-sex schools are at least not exposed to the awfulness of boys' behaviour, and this may be an overriding 'at least', there are several problems. First, as we have seen, girls' schools can be the poor relation when it comes to resources and facilities. It is amazing the extent to which they suddenly become aware of the facilities they lack when, on amalgamation, they become mixed schools. On the other hand, co-educational institutions may be bursting with resources but if girls never get access to them then the end result may be worse, for rather than never having had the opportunity to learn certain subjects they may have learnt that certain subjects were not for girls. Second, there is no guarantee that girls' schools are automatically geared towards helping their pupils become independent, autonomous human beings: 'Of course, single-sex education for girls can be used, and has been used in the past, to furnish girls with "accomplishments" suited only to a subordinate role in society.' (Spender and Sarah 1980.) On the other hand, girls are more likely to see women in positions of authority in girls' schools which must to some extent be a counter to such attitudes: 'I went to an all-girls school and most of my teachers were women. They were in positions of authority, they taught science and I never questioned the idea of women having careers and making decisions. It seemed quite normal to me.' (Spender and Sarah 1980.) Third, there is the danger that girls develop a totally idealized view of boys and are ill-prepared for the realities of life after school. This argument rests on three assumptions: the only contact which girls have with members of the opposite sex is in school; that co-education does prepare girls for the realities of life; and that only in mixed schools can a realistic view of boys be gained. All of these are false. Girls are surrounded with experience of males, in their families, in the media and in any public space. Co-education, except where there are specific anti-sexist initiatives, does not prepare girls – as one teacher said, 'It batters them.' Fourth, there is no reason why realistic views of boys should not be developed in girls' schools; the teacher who sent the lists of abusive words works in a girls' school. It may even be easier to discuss the problematic behaviour of boys in a girls' school. None of the arguments against girls' schools are highly convincing. However, when it comes to boys' schools the problem is rather more difficult.

It is often said that boys' schools reinforce masculinity much more strongly than mixed ones. This is hard to believe if it is true that identity as a male is conferred and confirmed by other males since in both situations other males are present. What may be true is that in boys' schools there is a total absence of challenge from girls and most of the few women staff occupy the lower positions of authority. Boys themselves apparently see the advantages of mixed schools as: '. . . less homosexuality (top of the list), getting on with girls, less pressure to conform to macho images. Staff would certainly agree that *there is less violence*' (EOC 1982; my emphasis). From this it is perhaps possible to theorize not that boys' schools construct masculinity more strongly but that it is reinforced in different ways. In mixed schools boys confirm their masculinity to each other through their behaviour towards girls, but in the absence of girls they may resort to physical violence to achieve their position in the male hierarchy. As boys get older and gain kudos from dating girls, they have to modify their behaviour to be acceptable at all, and as one teacher said: 'They transform macho aggression into a sort of suavity which is not so obviously violent.' That boys are so violently homophobic perhaps bears witness to the fact that they only see each other as masculine if their sexuality is being practised on girls.

Neither mixed schools for girls nor single-sex schools for boys are attractive propositions. This is because the basic problem, which as I have argued is the social construction of maleness, is yet to be tackled.

To argue that such challenge is more possible where girls are present rather gives the lie to their supposed status of passive victims.

The next step is to decide who will work with the boys. In the best of all possible worlds it probably ought not to be female teachers. First, which of us could bear to immerse ourselves for any length of time in what emerged when these men began working with boys: 'The subjects that emerged most strongly as the ones the boys wanted to engage with were those of physical violence. They were clearly very concerned with their own sexuality, and with themes related to this.' (Cornbleet and Sanders 1982.) Second, those best in a position to understand the experience of being constructed into masculinity are men. Third, the physical safety of women teachers might be more at risk than that of men's:

Norton Taylor mentioned three examples of behaviour from the boys' group that he felt might illuminate some of the difficulties of working with boys in a consciously anti-sexist way. Firstly, there were those boys who responded to discussions of sexist attitudes with vehement expressions of mysogynistic contempt and hatred. At one session of the boys' group the intensity of emotions was such that a boy started smashing windows in rage. (EOC 1982.)

One wonders what might have happened if a woman had been taking the session. However, although there is a strong case for male teachers to work with boys on an anti-sexist basis there are problems with this proposal. It has to be said that beyond complaining about exclusion from women's groups, male teachers have had a poor record when it comes to actually doing anything. Still, it remains to be seen whether anti-sexist men will take this opportunity to become centrally involved in anti-sexist work. Again, it is to be hoped that this work will be carried out with energy and commitment:

The male teachers did not feel able, within the confines of the school, to actively challenge and question (boys') assumptions. . . . Whilst feminist teachers are actively challenging and confronting pupils regarding their sexist prejudices all the time, it has to be said that the reluctance of men teachers to do the same inhibits the process of change and, on educational grounds, is insufficient. (Cornbleet and Sanders 1982.)

Even when commitment has been given, men may need help initially about how to organize their anti-sexist work with boys:

But the main constraint was our inability to give the boys access in school to the kind of material which many of them had access to outside school – to pornographic magazines, films and literature. . . .

At present these themes of violence and sexuality, and their fascination for sexually maturing boys, are largely ignored within the school. We believe that it will only be possible to tackle such themes when it becomes possible to consider with such boys the material (often of a violent or pornographic nature) which is available to them increasingly outside the school, and then attempting (in an undogmatic way) to deal with the issues such material raises for the same boys. (Cornbleet and Sanders 1982.)

Whatever else is involved in working with boys I find it difficult to stomach the idea that it necessitates the use of pornography in school.

It is important not to underestimate the difficulty of persuading boys to change for this amounts to asking them to give up power which guarantees the maintenance of a situation where: 'A man's comfort and well-being are contingent upon the labour and nurture of women.' (Stoltenberg 1977.) What arguments could be used to show boys that it is in their interest to change? Kate Myers suggests one which is that

traditional masculine values [are] synonymous with physical self-destruction:
1. taking as much pain as possible without giving in
2. being able to 'hold' alchohol
3. not showing feeling/showing emotion
4. being highly competitive and achievement orientated. (EOC 1982.)

The problem with this is that boys could be persuaded to give up the health hazards of being men without this in any way affecting how they related to women. In China a similar problem was encountered in persuading men that changed attitudes and behaviour to women was in their interests (Croll 1978):

If you are indifferent or opposed to women becoming skilled locomotive workers, you just don't know where your interests lie. Are you better off when you keep the women in your families in idleness? . . . If your womenfolk earn their living they both free themselves and you.

Men were further persuaded to the benefits of allowing their wives to work when it was pointed out that with the extra money 'their women-folk' would be able to buy new clothes! Being able to please your man, whether economically or in terms of 'attractiveness', is not from women's point of view the point of liberation at all.

Perhaps it would be better to acknowledge that it is not in men's interest to change, at least in the political sense of 'interest'. This does not mean that they ought not to. There is nothing to prevent men from rejecting on moral grounds a system from which at the same time they benefit. If some white feminists (lamentably few) have worked hard to try to eradicate their own racism, constructed by a racist society in their political interests, why should not men seek to eradicate their oppressive attitudes and behaviour towards women?

In the meantime, if anything is clear it is this: co-education as things stand is not more socially desirable for girls because it is more normal. Rather, because it is more normal it is, for girls, highly undesirable. This does not mean that girls' schools, just because boys are absent, have no need to look critically at the messages they convey about women (see Appendix 1). Nor does it mean that boys' schools, just because girls are absent, are inevitably building sites for the macho male (see Appendix 2). Enough work has now been undertaken for us to be able to say that change is possible and that teachers and pupils can make it happen (see Appendix 3). Since the girls and women in this study face the same world tomorrow as they did yesterday, such change is in my view a matter of some urgency. It is in this spirit that it is to be hoped that this conclusion represents a beginning.

Appendix 1

Yvonne Beecham, a social studies teacher and former advisory teacher for Inner London Education Authority, makes the following observations on possibilities for girls' schools (1984):

'Of course we don't need a school policy on equal opportunities, this is a girls' school.'

Within the next year all I.L.E.A. schools will be asked to submit their policies on Equal Opportunities re. Gender. Many teachers have already developed policies and guidelines for good practice, in some cases before I.L.E.A. officially recognized this as an area needing specific policy. Most of the work has been done in mixed schools. Girls' schools have tended to lag behind, perhaps because there are no boys around to engage in the many forms of sexual harassment.

In girls' schools it has tended to be classroom teachers who have taken up such issues as sexist curricula. Management, when they have recognized the issue, have focused on such things as providing more science and technical subjects. Science is promoted in the belief that it will help girls/young women get jobs and because it is seen as having high status.

Ideally a school's staff should start from some common understanding of the disadvantages faced by girls/women. This will rarely be the case in reality and those concerned with developing the policy will have to begin with basic discussion around the issues with other staff. Given a common starting point I would see the following issues as crucial in the development of anti-sexist guidelines in girls' schools.

Attempts must be made to remove sexist assumptions in the curriculum, and the dominance of knowledge which is only about men. It is not enough simply to add more male dominated subject areas to the curriculum. The curriculum must also reflect the cultural diversity of Britain today and lead to an awareness of the power relationships between the countries of the world.

This is preferable to introducing women's studies as a subject option. This simply provides an outlet for many teachers to say 'we don't need to change what we are doing because women's studies looks at the question'. There is also the issue of assessing how well girls do on women's studies courses if they are taught as an examinable or testable subject. What does it mean to 'fail' a women's studies course?

I would like to see a policy which re-values traditional women's skills and knowledge areas as well as encouraging the development in girls of new skill areas. Needlework, fabric and design, home economics etc. should encourage young women to enjoy doing things for themselves and to see that their own health and welfare is as important as that of others. Traditionally such subjects have promoted the culture of white middle-class families and this bias will need to be challenged.

In terms of introducing new areas to the curriculum I would like to see all girls undertake courses in Assertiveness training and self defence. This is crucial to the overall development of positive self-images of young women.

In order that anti-sexist teaching does not simply become a form of compensatory education it is vital that teachers have positive views of those they teach. Women teachers should provide positive role models for the young women both in themselves and by involving women in a meaningful way from the community. Strategies must also be developed for dealing with male teachers' resistance and harassment of girls. This must be backed up by the school administration, L.E.A.s and teachers' unions. Women teachers need to support each other and to encourage girls/young women to do the same.

For any school-based policy to be successful parental support and understanding is essential. The school needs to develop ways of informing parents of the aims of the policy and how it is working, and where possible involve them directly.

For any policy to be successful the school staffing structure should be assessed in terms of who holds the power, the sexual distribution of heads of department, senior teachers, etc. and non-teaching staff; if there is an imbalance then attempts must be made to rectify this by the L.E.A. How money is distributed throughout the school also needs to be looked at, while recognizing that there will always be dispute between teachers who see their own subjects as a priority.

Often teachers will complain that they cannot implement an anti-sexist policy without the aid of new teaching materials, but while some new materials are required (which teachers can produce themselves if given time), much of the existing materials can be used from a critical standpoint. Pupils are very quick to recognize the bias in existing textbooks once they have discussed and are aware of the issues.

I have not attempted here to provide a blue-print for an anti-sexist policy but merely to raise some background issues which must be discussed before a specific policy statement can be developed.

Fighting sexism in single-sex girls' schools should be as much a priority as changing mixed-sex schools and must go deeper than simply adding 'boys'' subjects to the curriculum.

Appendix 2

In spite of some reservations about what it means to 'lift' school policies out of the contexts and meanings of particular institutions and 'freeze' them and in spite of there being considerable debate about policy, it may be useful to have examples of two. Quinton Kynaston is a mixed school and Hackney Downs a boys' school, both in London.

Sex differentiation in school: a programme for change
(Quinton Kynaston School)

This item is based on work done by the Sex Differentiation Working Party over the last four years and on its recent conference attended by 18 QK staff, 3 Institute students, 3 School Council representatives and 1 parent.

1.0 *Rationale*
Our concern to offer all students the opportunity of equality needs to transform itself from words into action.

1.1 We have made little impact so far on uptake of 'non-stereotypical' subjects in the fourth and fifth year. Further when girls do opt for 'boys'' subjects they are more likely to fail than are boys.

In both 81 and 82 we ran an option choice programme specifically designed to help students make informed choices. We placed a lot of emphasis on avoiding sex stereotypes. Results show that intervention at that stage is not very effective.

In 83 we abandoned 'option pools' hoping to create them on the basis of student choice rather than pre-selecting. Initial analysis done by Caroline Lodge indicates, if anything, polarisation.

1.2 *Use of resources*
Time and money is not equally divided between girls and boys.
More boys than girls get:

learning support
option support
study centre support

Boys take up more 'pastoral' time than girls.

We spend more money on boys (cost of transport for matches etc. for boys far outweighs the costs for girls).

Boys gain more teacher attention and have greater access to talk than girls.

1.3   We have not gone far enough in reviewing our curriculum and changing it.

1.4   While many existing materials present derogatory images of women, too often homemade materials use similar art work.

Women, their experiences and achievements are almost always invisible. How many posters in departments show women at work? (Don't count the recent spate made by the Sex Differentiation Working Party.)

How much of what our students learn is about man at work, at war, in the laboratory, the workshop, in politics?

How much value is given to domestic labour and traditional female crafts?

2.0   *Focus for change*

We could spend hours in meetings telling each other what's going wrong and blaming everyone else for the problem. It's the parents, it's the primary school, it's the attitude of that group of teachers. It's everybody's problem. Everyone, that is, who has a serious commitment to comprehensive schooling and what that means in terms of equal access and support for all students.

What can we do *this year*? (83/84)

3.0   *Recommendations* (short term)

(a)   Give girls space. They need places to meet and talk without boys. One room on each floor to be allocated to girls. School Council to discuss and help implement.

(b)   Involve parents.

School Council have written a brochure 'QK – An Equal Opportunity School'. This to be given out at interviews for new students.

Use option choice and agreement sessions to sell the *whole* of our curriculum to girls and boys.

(c) Use single sex groupings.

Already developed in Sex Education units in SE. Extend to option choice programme.

Trial single sex groups in some options.

Separate girls' and boys' lunchtime/club/community activities in Maths, Computer Studies, Design Technology, Science – wherever there's a use of non-class time in a subject which is sex differentiated.

Trial single sex groups in Maths/Science/DT. Faculty to discuss.

(d) Draw up a *departmental policy* – publish it and work at it.

(e) *Curriculum review*

Central question – is this course accessible to all students regardless of initial ability skills (i.e. appropriate for Mixed Ability Teaching)

— does it allow experience of success for all students
— does its content focus too narrowly on male experience
— what changes can we make?

We have now got contacts with subject specialists experienced in work on sex differentiation. The WP will be offering to arrange workshops to all departments this term.

Materials/image

What do our rooms, books, materials tell students about who studies this subject? What can we do about that message?

Asking the questions

Do moderation and review reports focus on sex differentiation? (only 2 review reports mentioned the topic last year).

Develop specific materials/programmes

In each subject area which give value to women and their experience, which show the contribution of women to that subject.

(f) Offer active support to all students. The non-macho boy probably gets more teasing than the assertive girl.

(g) *Act* on QK policy on sexual abuse – question student attitudes, refer problems.

(h) Extend the debate and action into primary link schools. Build on their progress, share our experience.

4.0 *Recommendations* (long term)

Our development of core curriculum in years 4 and 5 is very significant. We should look to that to help us define what is essential learning for all students.

SE Course development teams should start work across the curriculum on parenthood education.

We should add our voices to current requests for crèches and appropriate paternity leave, as well as maternity allowances.

A policy for sex equity and anti-sexism in Hackney Downs

Introductory

Examples of the promotion of equal opportunities and of anti-sexist initiatives within schools have sprung mainly from all-girls' schools or co-educational establishments. Hackney Downs is – at present – an all boys' school, which collaborates at the 16–19 age level with girls from Clapton and Hackney Free.

While not denying the massive evidence of unequal opportunities for girls in education, nor minimising the seriousness of sexist behaviour, attitudes and language which threaten and assault females in this school, our pupils are also victims of sex stereotypical roles. Neither the overt nor the covert curriculum of Hackney Downs has yet taken up or acted upon these issues in much depth or consistent commitment.

One major problem which at the moment has been responded to by the Skills for Living working party, is the paucity of provision of education for sexual self-definition, relationships between the sexes, parenthood and domestic responsibility. Socially formed attitudes to women and work are part of the problem; there IS a stereotyped male ethos in the school and we wish to encourage initiatives to counter this and set out a clearer statement of policy and positive structures for lines of action.

A policy for sex equity and anti-sexism is a whole school policy, in the same way our commitment to multi-ethnic education is a whole school policy. Just as anti-racism is not the responsibility only of black members of our community, neither is anti-sexism the responsibility only of the Women's Group and the female members of staff.

Fairness to both sexes is the basic principle which should inform our policy and our practice. This involves action which is positive in redressing our rejection of sex stereotyping and sexism.

This requires of us:

(a) a shared understanding by all staff of the nature of sex stereotyping and sexism;
(b) consensus among us about the desirability of change and about methods;

(c) commitment to carrying through positive changes over a period of time, to monitoring and reappraisal;

(d) commitment to continuing anti-sexist action;

(e) resources, particularly time, for all to work out the implications of their own role and for discussion with others;

(f) the formulation, adoption and implementation of a written policy for sex equity and anti-sexism which is a whole school policy.

School policy on sex equity and anti-sexism

1 Issues of sexism are taken seriously and are dealt with as we expect issues of racism to be dealt with. (Our normal procedures include a personal response on the spot; supporting and being supported by colleagues who are nearby; discussion with the offenders; consultation with form tutors, Heads of Department, Heads of House; selection of appropriate follow-up for individuals or whole classes by those most likely to be effective – female and male.)

(a) Incidents of sexual violence, verbal and physical, are responded to immediately, from a sense of collective responsibility.

(b) Expressions of sexist attitudes and opinions do not pass unheard. As a whole staff we make an overt stand on principle against sexism.

(c) To gauge the extent and nature of the problem we kept a record of all such incidents for at least one term.

2 There should be in-service training available for staff on anti-sexist education.

3 Departments (including the Library and Media Resources) will examine materials and resources for sexist content and look for ways to redress the balance.

4 Positive anti-sexist content will be in current courses, especially in Careers, Craft, Humanities and Science. The range of extra-curricular activity will be examined for similar anti-sexist activity; we could try to organise group activities which include girls from other schools, or encourage interest in events, outings, exhibitions etc. beyond the stereotypical 'boys only' ones.

5 Heads of House and Heads of Department will ensure that issues of sex equity and anti-sexism are on their meeting agendas at least once a term. This includes form tutor meetings and department meetings.

6   The Curriculum Study Group will examine the whole curriculum with reference to sex equity and anti-sexism in the courses on offer and selection of options. They will consider ways to redress any imbalance, and report to the staff, parents and governors.

7(a)   Anti-sexist and sex equitable initiatives will be encouraged and supported. Cross-curricular areas like the Library and Media Resources department may need particular support, but as a whole school we could also initiate moves concerning display material around school, film hire, visiting speakers, and theatre companies, and publishing within the school.

(b)   Financial resources will be allocated to anti-sexist and sex equitable initiatives. (As in the past we have funded initiatives on issues of class, race and language, which are continuing.)

Dealing with incidents of sexual assault

Hackney Downs School is inexperienced at handling such incidents. It was felt necessary to focus on the issues and problems separately from other incidents of assault. It is important that we become confident and aware, so that effective action can be taken. These notes refer to cases where the assailant is identified.

Sexual assault is an aspect of women's experience in an all boys' school and some men find it difficult to see any difference between a sexual assault and other forms of assault suffered by staff. It is an act of violence against a person, it is an act of deliberate hostility which focuses on the sexual organs of the victim to demean and humiliate. It is this intention which distinguishes sexual assault from other forms of physical contact – the hostile ones which inflict physical hurt, the friendly ones which communicate caring.

Victims of sexual assault will be supported without question, on the assumption that no one makes up that kind of accusation. Once the victim has reported the incident she will not be called upon to give a public account of it again unless she wishes to do so; the Head, Deputy or House Tutor will intercede for and represent the victim. Should it be a case ending in a suspension and a governors' hearing the Head will represent the victim's case unless she prefers to do so herself.

Members of staff dealing with pupil (and parent) over the case must take great care in discussing it.

1. Do not get into an argument about exactly what happened. A sexual assault is a sexual assault.
2. Pupil and parent must be informed clearly and unambiguously that Hackney Downs School will not condone sexual assault.
3. Discussion must deal with the issues: e.g.
   — a woman's body is not 'fair game' to be grabbed at
   — women are people and workers, NOT inferior beings or sex objects
   — no person has any right to force themselves on another person's body. . . .

Those who commit sexual assault will be punished and must be seen to be punished. Although no one standard punishment may suit every case (particularly at this stage of Hackney Downs School getting its procedures clear) the seriousness of the offence must be made clear. At this stage a gentle telling off is not enough; there is a need for the school to assert its values. The problem for the school is that the values which oppose sexual assault also oppose some mainstream values of the stereotyped male ethos of an all boys' school.

Appendix 3

The past six years of anti-sexist work at Stoke Newington School are reviewed by Sue Libovitch and Annie Cornbleet.

Report on anti-sexist initiatives at Stoke Newington School

Introduction
In this report we shall be looking at both the positive and negative aspects of the initiatives undertaken during the past six years. This involves the following three main areas:

1 The History of Anti-Sexist Initiatives in Stoke Newington School.
2 Review of Present Practice and Attitudes based on the Questionnaire, discussion and general comments.
3 Proposals for Staff Policy 84/85 (Green Paper).

1 *The history of anti-sexist initiatives in Stoke Newington School*

1978/79 The play 'It's A Hard Life Being A Girl' – written and performed by fourth year girls and taken into schools and theatres, for both girls only and mixed audiences. Parts of it were used in a film distributed by Cinema of Women entitled 'Taught To Be Girls'.

1979/82 Formation of Anti-Sexist Working Party. Wrote a report out of which school policy was formulated at a staff meeting. Report also went to the Governors and accepted.

1980/81 Single Sex Assertiveness Training Programme for third year pupils. This was in tutor time, for half an hour per week and depended on the goodwill of colleagues.
Single Sex Sex Education and Personal Development Courses for 1st and 2nd years.
Appointment of Senior Teacher for Equal Opps. (Clissold Park School).
Resignation of Anti-Sexist Working Party.

1981/82   D.A.S.I. Project – School Focused Inservice Training Project (Developing Anti-Sexist Initiatives) supported by ILEA and EOC (See Report & Resources Booklet).
Amalgamation of Clissold Park School and Wodberry Down Schools into Stoke Newington School.
Formation of Women's Group S N School.
Removal of Senior Teacher Post for Equal Opps. from staffing structure.

1982/83   Single Sex first year Foundation Course:
'Sex Role Stereotyping Unit' written by Annie Cornbleet and Sue Libovitch specifically for this course. For the first time it was recognised that every new pupil at the school would have one double lesson per week in single sex groups with a teacher of their own sex. Second Unit also written and taught entitled 'Mirrors of Romance and A Touch of Broken Glass'.
Inservice Training for the teachers committed to the teaching of the above unit.
Single Sex Counselling.
Assertiveness training in third year.
Careers Convention – highlighting the counteracting of sex role stereotyping.
Single Sex Extra Curricular activities.
Option Choices.
Setting Up of Anti-Sexist Resources Room.
Girls Only Space – inside and outside the school building.
Girls Club.
Also Single Sex Groups:
   Physics – fourth year
   Maths – fourth year
   Social Skills – fourth year.
   D & T – fourth, first and second year.
   Drama – All years.

1983/84   first year – Single Sex lessons teaching the units – fully integrated into the main core of the curriculum.
   – Twice weekly optional choice of entering a single sex group for Maths or French.
   – Inservice sessions for teachers of above units.
   second year – Single Sex Groups in English and Maths.
   Some practical subjects in first and second years have an all boys group in order to redress the numerical imbalance in the ratio of boys to girls (which is approx. 3 to 1).

third year – Single Sex Assertiveness Training.
fourth year – Single Sex Maths and Physics Groups.
   Careers & Option Choices geared to non-stereotypical outcomes.
fifth year – Single sex groups in:
   Social Studies
   Maths
   English
   Community Service
   Computers
   – Individual and group counselling.
   – College and job advice attempting to expand opportunities.

An application was made to the Inservice Training Section of ILEA, but funding was refused as work was already on-going. However, an application to the Girls Education Fund was favourably received and we now have approximately £2,600 for resources to further our work. For the first time, departments will have specific resources for girls and there is money available to pass teachers for girls activities after school.

2   *Review of present practice and attitudes based on the questionnaire, discussions and general comments*

This section is subdivided into three main areas:
(a)   Subject areas
(b)   Pastoral work
(c)   General ethos of the school

(a)   *Subject areas*
Most subject areas perceived great problems with the existing materials available. The following are writing and producing their own anti-sexist materials:

   English, Home Economics, Learning Development, Maths, French,
   Business Studies, Social Studies

Single sex grouping was seen favourably by most departments if it could be resourced properly and seen as part of the curriculum. French, English, Science, Social Studies and Integrated Studies all had very strong positive feelings about their single sex groups. This covered the age range from years one to five. The Maths department was divided. Women Maths teachers stated their approval and positive reaction to the all girls groups. The male Head of Department was steering away from this idea as he felt that the resulting all boys groups were impossible and that the girls were alienated by it. He found it much more successful to team teach with one teacher giving special attention to the girls in the mixed group. The debate continues in this area but school policy which favours single sex teaching must be borne in mind, as well as the opinions of women members of the department. Science and Design and Technology felt that more ought to be done to counteract stereotypical choices and attitudes in this area. Both advised single sex work and both wanted more resources for girls. Science does have a policy in this and creates single sex physics and chemistry groups whenever possible. Currently, there is a fourth form Chemistry group comprising seventeen girls, taught by a woman teacher, on the Woodberry Down site.

In general most subjects saw the need to discuss this issue more at departmental meetings and give it a higher status and priority with resourcing.

(b) *Pastoral work*

The house systems, year sections and mini-schools all complained that it was almost impossible to counteract the dominant ratio of boys to girls within tutoring. One viable solution, at Woodberry Down, was to create an all girls registration group. Each pastoral section made time and space for girls and commented that this gave girls confidence, a chance to explore personal problems with increased trust and made possible more work on option choices and job advice.

For the purpose of this report we are including personal development, tutoring and job advice under the heading of pastoral work. Below are the most commonly expressed favourable comments:

Girls' single sex groups encourage much fuller, better discussion of a whole range of topics.

Some house systems saw a direct improvement in the girls' assertiveness and in their challenging of male intimidation.

In one section at Woodberry Down, after school sessions for girls were held as this appeared to be the only time available for tutors to spend uninterrupted time with their girl students.

The girls were given link courses in Mechanics and Electronics plus work experience in these areas which crossed stereotypical boundaries and gave girls much confidence.

The third year team noted more articulate criticism by the girls about their feelings after single sex work.

Girls were much more reluctant to accept aggressive physical behaviour from boys. Girls were more openly critical in general of the education they are being offered. This may make them a problem in school generally, i.e. their new assertiveness may lead them into conflict with both individuals and the structure of the school.

The fourth year team reported some tutorial work in single sex groups for option talks, career talks and personal problems. Girls were suspicious at first, but see the importance of these issues now.

The second year team have implemented positive discrimination and have seen the importance of single sex groupings. They feel that there is more confidence on the part of the girls although this diminishes when boys are present.

Last year's fifth year team (Clissold Park site) reported a greater response by the girls to the general running and decision-making processes of the mixed class. Single sex counselling work generated a good bond between women teachers and girls.

Single sex work was particularly good for sex education and job advice.

However, there was a recognition that employing single sex groups alone did not automatically result in a solidarity amongst and between the girls.

Girls belonging to minority ethnic groups are being discriminated against because all of us fail to recognise feminism in other cultures. We need to listen, learn and incorporate these multi-faith and multi-cultural ideas of feminism into all our anti-sexist teaching.

Most male teachers felt that not enough was being done for the boys although they did not feel that they should be the ones to make the initiatives in this area. Some men (by far the minority) saw that they needed to take a more active role in changing sexist attitudes. Fewer still actively challenged the sexist viewpoints of boy students and did not confront their male colleagues. Some felt they needed to have different kinds of material and discussions with boys but thought that boys only groups were difficult. It is obvious that men who are challenging and trying to change sexist attitudes are isolated and they have considered forming a men's group. The women's group would welcome such a move. Most male teachers only want to react to sexist behaviour, not prevent it.

The boys' behaviour in general was not commented on beyond saying that their attitudes had stayed much the same; only when the girls had demanded a change in boys' behaviour did they consider 'sexism'.

(c) *General ethos of the school*

One great failure of the school as a community is in its inability to fully include the non-teaching staff in areas of concern for the pupils and in decision making. This is the fault of the teachers within the school who fail to recognise the impact that the non-teaching staff have on the pupils in their attitudes towards sexism. It is a fundamental principle of feminism to challenge hierarchical structures and whilst we acknowledge that the position and power of the non-teaching staff is not the same as the teachers, we would hope that in future any groups who form to combat sexism would include a genuine cross-section of all those who work in the school. At the same time, it would be anomalous to have one person 'in charge' of anti-sexist work as there can be no experts and no one individual is responsible for an issue that concerns us all so greatly. Hopefully, there will be a guaranteed commitment from all members of staff and those who feel especially interested would form a new working collective.

Most answers to the questionnaire showed that the staff certainly have a consciousness about language, and about spoken, written and visual material. With regard to sexual harassment the staff saw the need to tackle aggressive behaviour. However, the implicit threatening attitudes of the boys was not readily acknowledged, and a certain collusion operates to the benefit of those members of staff not prepared to tackle this issue.

The following proposals aim to help prevent this process of collusion. They also build on the lessons learnt from our struggles and make solid foundations for the future of anti-sexist theory and practice.

3   *Proposals for staff policy 84/85 (Green Paper)*

(i)   Subject areas
- (a)   Each subject area should look at their materials for sexism and wherever possible produce specifically anti-sexist resources which also include an active recognition of girls from multi-faith cultures.
- (b)   Single sex groups should be established to encourage girls to work together and to give them the space and attention denied them in mixed classes. This could be for an examination subject for two years or once a week for any subject area.
- (c)   Anti-sexist posters and girls' work should be displayed in every teachers' room.
- (d)   Department should discuss and monitor the progress of girls and of their anti-sexist initiatives.

(ii)   Pastoral work
- (a)   Single sex tutoring groups should be encouraged where the ratio of boys to girls is obviously too difficult to counteract.
- (b)   Single sex work should be part of the tutorial system.

(c)   Decision making girls' groups should be set up to monitor and to suggest areas of change.

(d)   A girls' space should be created in each pastoral area for work with pupil and teacher and between pupils. A recent demand from girls on a school journey to have single sex activities and time during their time away should be acted upon.

(e)   Counter-stereotypical job advice should be given as well as encouragement to take up options.

(f)   Work experience and training should be given to girls wherever possible in non-stereotypical areas.

(g)   In service training should be given to tutors in how to deal with sexist behaviour and anti-sexist initiatives in general.

(iii)   General ethos

Stoke Newington School should work towards creating an ethos and atmosphere where girls and women can walk and talk without intimidation. To achieve this end we must ensure that:

(a)   Girls' space is given inside and outside the building and is supervised in the manner of any other break time area.

(b)   Male teachers should stop using their voices and bodies to hold power against women and girls.

(c)   Sexist language should be acted upon and in the case of male teachers and boys, disciplinary procedures taken where necessary.

(d)   The physical abuse of girls should be severely dealt with; exclusion for three days and the parents seen and in the more serious cases of attack, expulsion.

(e)   Girls should be listened to and their word accepted when complaints are made about sexist behaviour.

In conclusion

These proposals should be discussed at a staff meeting entirely given over to anti-sexism within Stoke Newington School. Each proposal should be voted on and those with a majority vote should be accepted as school policy. The accepted proposals should be monitored and a new report written at the end of the next academic year.

This report is by no means complete nor is it prepared by an 'authority' on anti-sexist initiatives. It is part of an on-going process which must be kept at the forefront of our minds.

Notes

Chapter 1   Preparing the ground: some general observations on sexism and education

1   As Jill Lavigueur points out not all arguments in favour of co-education have stemmed from what feminists would regard as a progressive spirit:

> A belief in the complementary needs of the two sexes is central to the argument in favour of co-education put forward in the course of extensive research on the subject by R. R. Dale. Like all others who have held this view, including Newsom, he sees women as complementing the qualities of men rather than vice versa, the feminine role being the more passive and subordinate one. (Lavigueur 1980.)

Chapter 2   A can of worms: the sexual harassment of girls by boys

1   Later I talked to a teacher in a newly amalgamated school. Two schools, one girls' and the other boys' were put together to form one school which was named after a woman. He said: 'The boys hate it – they refuse to use it – they call the school by the old boys' school name.' I asked him what the girls' reaction was. 'Fine – no trouble.'

Chapter 3   Natural predators?: yet another critique of biological explanation

1   Those readers who are at this point experiencing a volcanic yawn, having concluded many years ago, along with much feminist literature, that biological differences per se between girls and boys explain little about the oppression of women, are invited to proceed forthwith to the next chapter.

Chapter 4   Parasite and host: capitalism and patriarchy, which is which?

1   Dale Spender (1981) draws attention to the fact that in common with many other studies, girls were entirely excluded from this one. She goes on:

> . . . the response of some researchers has been to provide 'explanations' for their

exclusion of women – sometimes in the form of a footnote! . . . If we are to accept the explanation proffered by Halsey et al then the future looks bleak for women for they gave as their reason for the exclusion of women the fact that they had not been included in past studies. In such a way the structural exclusion of women is used to justify the continued structural exclusion of women.

2 This assumption is not limited to Western culture. Khomeini's beliefs on this aspect of male sexuality lead him to recommend women as the main object of satisfaction for men though 'youths and camels are discussed as secondary sources' (Afshar 1982).

3 There is a problem about what to call it. 'Social maleness' or 'masculinity' is all too cosy; as 'something out there' it can all too easily become the subject of academic debate for men without them taking responsibility for deconstructing it, or for its effects on women or for the ways they benefit as a group irrespective of the degree to which they display it. On the other hand in citing the problem as one of 'men' often results in a great deal of tedious debate about whether one is or is not a biological determinist (really). Just as the space between 'white people' and 'white racism' is a space for change, likewise it seems most politic to create such a space between 'biological maleness' and 'social maleness'.

4 There is a rather persistent question which recurs in relation to this. 'Why should men want to control women?' The question is ambiguous; if it means 'How did it all begin?' then the answer is we do not know, although Merlin Stone (1979) has an interesting thesis. On the other hand if we mean 'Why should they want to continue?', then as Scarlet Friedmann says: '. . . why does any group or class of people oppress any other group? That is to say, why is history a history of the domination and subordination of social groups? Why does any ruling class exploit the subordinate class to its own ends?'

Bibliography

Achilles Heel (December 1982), Sexuality Issue

Afshar, H. (1981), 'The position of women in an Iranian village', *Feminist Review*, **9**

Afshar, H. (1982), 'Khomeini's teachings and the implications for women', *Feminist Review*, **12**

Althusser, L. (1971), 'Ideology and ideological state apparatuses', in Althusser, *Lenin and other Essays*, London: New Left Books

BBC2, 'Horizon' (1979), 'The Fight to be Male'

BBC2, 'A Question of Equality: Gender' (1981)

Beaton, I. (1860), *Book of Household Management*, London: Jonathan Cape

Bowles, S. and Gintis, H. (1976), *Schooling in Capitalist America*, London: Routledge & Kegan Paul

Brina, M. (1981), 'Sexism in education', Unpublished paper

Butler, M. and Paisley, W. (1979), *Women and the Mass Media*, Human Services Press

Carabin, E. and Dodd, M. (1982), 'All in a day's work', Unpublished paper

Clarricoates, K. (1978), 'The theft of girls creativity', Unpublished paper

Clarricoates, K. (1980), 'The importance of being Ernest . . . Emma . . . Tom . . . Jane . . .', in R. Deem (ed.), *Schooling for Women's Work*, London: Routledge & Kegan Paul

Cornbleet, A. and Sanders, S. (1982), *Designing Anti-Sexist Initiatives*, London: Inner London Education Authority/Equal Opportunities Commission

Coveney, L. *et al*. (1984), *The Sexuality Papers: Male sexuality and the social control of women*, London: Hutchinson

Croll, E. (1978), *Feminism and Socialism in China*, London: Routledge & Kegan Paul

Dale, R. (1975), 'Education and sex roles', *Educational Review*, 22 no. 3

Daly, M. (1979), *Gynaecology*, London: The Women's Press

Deem, R. (1978), *Women and Schooling*, London: Routledge & Kegan Paul

Deere, C. and de Leal, M. (1981), 'Peasant production, proletarianisation and the sexual division of labour', *Signs*, 7 no. 2

Dyhouse, C. (1978), 'Towards a feminine curriculum for English schoolgirls', *Women's Studies International Quarterly*, 1 no. 4

El Sadaawi, N. (1980), *The Hidden Face of Eve*, London: Zed Press

Equal Opportunities Commission/National Union of Teachers (1980), *Promotion and the Woman Teacher*

Equal Opportunities Commission (1981), *Fifth Annual Report*

Equal Opportunities Commission (1982), *What's in it for Boys?*

Firestone, S. (1979), *Dialectic of Sex*, London: The Women's Press

Fisher, E. (1979), *Woman's Creation*, New York: McGraw Hill

Friedmann, S. (1982), 'Heterosexuality, couples and parenthood: a natural cycle', in Friedmann and Sarah (eds.), *On the Problem of Men*

Friedmann, S. and Sarah, E. (eds.) (1982), *On the Problem of Men*, London: the Women's Press

Griffiths, V. (1977), 'Sex roles in the secondary school', Unpublished paper

Gubb, J. (1980), 'Language and role in mixed sex groups', *Language for Learning*, 2 no. 1

Hacker, S. and Schneider, J. (1972), 'Sex role imagery and the use of the generic man in introductory texts', Unpublished paper

Halsey, A., Heath, A. and Ridge, J. (1980), *Origins and Destinations*, Oxford: Oxford University Press

Hartmann, H. (1979), 'The unhappy marriage of marxism and feminism', *Capital and Class*, 8

Heider, K. (1976), 'Dani sexuality: a low energy system', *Man*, 11 no. 2

Hemmings, S. (1982), *Girls Are Powerful*, London: Sheba

Hooks, B. (1981), *Ain't I a Woman*, London: South End Press

Horner, M. (1972), 'Towards an understanding of achievement related conflicts in women', *Journal of Social Issues*, 28

Horrocks, L. (1984), 'Strong and silent?', Unpublished paper

Hull, G., Scott, P. and Smith, B. (1979), *All the Women are White, All the Men are Black, But Some of Us are Brave*, New York: Feminist Press

Inner London Education Authority (1981), 'Achievement in Schools', *Contact* (6 November 1981)

Jackson, M. (1983), 'Sexual liberation or social control?', *Women's Studies International Forum*, 6 no. 1

Jackson, M. (1984), 'Sex research and the construction of sexuality: a tool of male supremacy?', *Women's Studies International Forum*, 7 no. 1

Jackson, S. (1978), *On the Social Construction of Female Sexuality*, Women's Research and Resources Centre

Jeffreys, S. (1983), *Sex Reform and Anti-Feminism in the 1920s in London Feminist History Group The Sexual Dynamics of History*, London: Pluto Press

Jeffreys, S. (1984), ' "Free from all uninvited touch of man": women's campaigns around sexuality 1880–1914', in Coveney *et al.*, *The Sexuality Papers*, London: Hutchinson

Jones, C. (1984), 'Sexual tyranny in mixed schools: an in depth study of male violence in one secondary school', in G. Weiner (ed.), *Just a Bunch of Girls: Feminist Approaches to Schooling*, Open University

Lavigueur, J. (1980), 'Co-education and the tradition of separate needs,' in Spender and Sarah (eds.), *Learning to Lose*

Leonard, D. (1977), 'Opportunities and choice in the curriculum', Unpublished paper

Litewka, J. (1977), 'The socialised penis', in Snodgrass, *For Men Against Sexism*

MacDonald, M. (1981), 'Schooling and the reproduction of class and gender relations', in R. Dale, G. Esland and M. MacDonald (eds.), *Education and the State*, vol. 2, Lewes: Falmer Press

McKinnon, C. (1979), *Sexual Harassment of Working Women*, London and New Haven: Yale University Press

McRobbie, A. and McCabe, T. (1981), *Feminism for Girls*, London: Routledge & Kegan Paul

Mahony, P. (1982), 'Silence in a woman's glory', *Women's Studies International Forum*, 5 no. 5

Mahony, P. (1983), 'Boys will be boys: teaching women's studies in mixed sex groups', *Women's Studies International Forum*, 6 no. 3

Mead, M. (1935), *Sex and Temperament in 3 Primitive Societies*, New York: Mentor

Mead, M. (1950), *Male and Female*, Harmondsworth: Penguin

Molyneux, M. (1981), 'Women in socialist societies', *Feminist Review*, 8

Moraga, C. and Anzaldua, G. (1981), *This Bridge called my Back*, Massachusetts: Persephone Press

Morris, J. (1974), *Conundrum*, London: Faber & Faber

Moys, M. (1980), *Modern Languages Examinations at 16+*, London: Centre for Information on Language Teaching Research

Newsom, J. (1963), *Half Our Future*, London: HMSO

Nicholas, J. (1983), *Issues in Comparative Education*, London: Harper & Row

Nilsen, A. (1972), 'Sexism in English: a feminist view', *Female Studies*, 6

Postlethwaite, K. and Denton, C. (1980), *Streams for the Future. Final Report of the Banbury Grouping Enquiry*, London: National Foundation for Educational Research

Oakley, A. (1972), *Sex, Gender and Society*, London: Temple Smith

Okin, S. (1980), *Women in Western Political Thought*, London: Virago

Raymond, J. (1980), *The Transsexual Empire*, London: The Women's Press

Raynor, R. (1984), 'The death of the permissive society', *Time Out* (1 March 1984)

Raynor, R. (1984), 'The sexual backlash', *Time Out* (8 March 1984)

Roberts, H. (ed.) (1981), *Women, Health and Reproduction*, London: Routledge & Kegan Paul

Rossi, A. (ed.) (1970), *Essays in Sex Equality*, Chicago: University of Chicago Press

Rubin, G. (1975), 'The traffic in women', in R. Reiter (ed.), *Toward an Anthropology of Women*, New York: Monthly Review Press

Sanday, P. (1981), *Female Power and Male Dominance*, Cambridge: Cambridge University Press

Sandra, M. (1982), *Teaching London Kids*, no. 19

Sayers, J. (1982), *Biological Politics*, London: Tavistock Publications

Schein, L. (1977), 'All men are misogynists', in Snodgrass (ed.), *For Men Against Sexism*

Schools Council (1981), 'Reducing sex differences in school', *Newsletter*, no. 1

Sharpe, S. (1976), *Just Like a Girl*, Harmondsworth: Penguin

Snodgrass, J. (ed.) (1977), *For Men Against Sexism*, Albion, Calif.: Times Change Press

Spare Rib (1983), 'Sexual harassment of girls and women teachers', *Spare Rib*, no. 131

Spector-Person, E. (1980), 'Sexuality as the mainstay of identity', *Signs*, 5 no. 4

Spender, D. (1978), 'Don't talk, listen', *TES* (3 November 1978)

Spender, D. (1980), *Man Made Language*, London: Routledge & Kegan Paul

Spender, D. (ed.) (1981), *Men's Studies Modified*, Oxford: Pergammon

Spender, D. (1982), *Invisible Women*, London: Writers and Readers Co-op

Spender, D. and Sarah, E. (eds.) (1980), *Learning to Lose*, London: The Women's Press

Stanworth, M. (1983), *Gender and Schooling: A study of sexual divisions in the classroom*, London: Hutchinson

Stoltenberg, J. (1977), 'Refusing to be a man', in Snodgrass (ed.), *For Men Against Sexism*

Stone, M. (1979), *The Paradise Papers*, London: Virago

Sutton, J. and Friedmann, S. (1982), 'Fatherhood: bringing it all back home', in Friedmann and Sarah (eds.), *On the Problem of Men*

Taylor, H. (1984), 'Reflection on the role of policy', Unpublished paper

Terman, L. and Miles, C. (1936), *Sex and Personality*, New York: McGraw Hill

TES (1983a), 'Continuing fall in number of women who become heads'

TES (1983b), 'The micro fanatics', *TES* (4 November 1983)

TES (1984a), 'ILEA finds women staff are paid less than men', *TES* (20 January 1984)

TES (1984b), 'Upsurge in women heads', *TES* (3 February 1984)

TES (1984c), 'Still puzzling over the sex equation', *TES* (17 February 1984)

WEDG (1983a), *Newsletter*, June

WEDG (1983b), *Newsletter*, October

WEDG (1984), 'Reflections on policy', Unpublished paper

Wildy, N., Howe, S., Crosbie, P., Collins, R. and Berman, P. (1984), 'Five go wandering: the unhappy marriage of gender and amalgamations', Unpublished paper

Willis, P. (1977), *Learning to Labour*, London: Saxon House

Wilson, E. (1983), *What's to be Done about Violence Against Women?*, Harmondsworth: Penguin

Wilson, E. O. (1975), *Sociobiology: The New Synthesis*, Harvard: Harvard University Press

Wolpe, A.-M. (1977), *Some Processes in Sexist Education*, Women's Research and Resources Centre

Wolpe, A.-M. (1978), *Feminism and Materialism*, London: Routledge & Kegan Paul

Wood, J. (1982), 'Boys will be boys', *New Socialist*, 5

Zaretsky, E. (1976), *Capitalism, the Family and Personal Life*, London: Pluto Press

Zimmerman, D. and West, C. (1975), 'Sex roles, interruptions and silences in conversation', in B. Thorne and N. Henley (eds.), *Language and Sex*, Massachusetts: Newbury House

For Product Safety Concerns and Information please contact our EU representative GPSR@taylorandfrancis.com Taylor & Francis Verlag GmbH, Kaufingerstraße 24, 80331 München, Germany

Batch number: 08153778

Printed by Printforce, the Netherlands